POINTS OF LIGHT

POINTS OF LIGHT

New Approaches to Ending Welfare Dependency

Gertrude Himmelfarb ◆ William Raspberry

Nicholas Lemann ◆ Mickey Kaus

Lawrence M. Mead ◆ Charles Murray

Ken Auletta ◆ Myron Magnet ◆ Judson Bemis

Editors, *The Washington Monthly*

Edited by
Tamar Ann Mehuron

Foreword by
Robert Woodson

ETHICS AND PUBLIC POLICY CENTER

The **ETHICS AND PUBLIC POLICY CENTER,** established in 1976, conducts a program of research, writing, publications, and conferences to encourage debate on domestic and foreign policy issues among religious, educational, academic, business, political, and other leaders. A nonpartisan effort, the Center is supported by contributions (which are tax deductible) from foundations, corporations, and individuals. The authors alone are responsible for the views expressed in Center publications.

Library of Congress Cataloging-in-Publication Data

Points of light : new approaches to ending welfare
dependency / Gertrude Himmelfarb ... [et al.] : edited by
Tamar Ann Mehuron : foreword by Robert Woodson.
p.   cm.
Includes index.
1. Public welfare—United States.   2. United States—
Social policy—1980–   I. Mehuron, Tam.
II. Himmelfarb, Gertrude.   III. Ethics and Public
Policy Center (Washington, D.C.)
HV95.P65   1990
361.6'0973   90–44277 CIP

ISBN 0–89633–151–2
ISBN 0–89633–152–0 (pbk.)

Distributed by arrangement with:
University Press of America, Inc.
4720 Boston Way
Lanham, MD 20706

3 Henrietta Street
London WC2E 8LU England

All Ethics and Public Policy Center books are produced on acid-free paper. The paper used in this publication meets the minimum requirements of American National Standard for Information Sciences—Permanence of Paper for Printed Library Materials, ANSI Z39.48–1984.   ∞™

Ethics and Public Policy Center
1030 Fifteenth Street N.W.
Washington, D.C. 20005
(202) 682–1200

Defenseless under the night
Our world in stupor lies;
Yet, dotted everywhere,
Ironic points of light
Flash out wherever the Just
Exchange their messages:
May I, composed like them
Of Eros and of dust
Beleaguered by the same
Negation and despair
Show an affirming flame.
　　　　　—W. H. AUDEN

From "September 1, 1939"

Contents

Foreword

Robert Woodson

Americans are a compassionate people. We care about the poor, the elderly, the handicapped, and persons who have suffered misfortune. Earlier this century, we expressed such concern through the extended family, religious organizations, and local community organizations. Then came the Great Depression in the 1930s, and President Franklin Roosevelt initiated, with the support of Congress and the Supreme Court, a series of federal programs designed to care for the unemployed and others in special need. Gradually America became a welfare state. But in recent years we have realized that throwing money at "the welfare problem" is not the complete answer and, in fact, is often a part of the problem. The net impact of the great variety of welfare programs has been to increase dependency rather than to decrease it.

We are all concerned with reducing poverty and with the dignity of the poor. We want the poor to move from poverty to productivity and self-respect. When President George Bush speaks of "a thousand points of light," he is referring to the many initiatives by individuals, religious institutions, private non-profit groups, businesses, and other organizations that are meeting the needs of people at the local level.

Since the War on Poverty launched in the 1960s, we have learned many lessons. Among them is the reality that the vast majority of

Robert Woodson is president of the National Center for Neighborhood Enterprise in Washington, D.C.

those on welfare do not wish to be. But one of the tragedies is that the welfare system is currently structured so that there is no "ladder" out of the canyon of dependency.

There are other lessons we have learned as well. The private sector can do a great deal more than we thought possible. In some cases, private efforts combined with state and federal government programs have done imaginative work in empowering people from welfare dependence to self-respect and self-sufficiency. Underlying such efforts is the realization that government cannot do it all; local programs that emphasize interpersonal relationships and aggressive market-oriented strategies for dealing with the welfare-dependent stand a much better chance of success.

Points of Light: New Approaches to Ending Welfare Dependency deals with the limits of government programs and advocates greater emphasis on private initiatives. Given the urgent need to combat the ills that afflict the underclass and the welfare-poor, it is imperative that we discover new approaches that are compassionate and that restore and uphold the dignity and self-respect of all Americans. This timely and insightful volume presents a cogent discussion of the complexities and challenges facing both the welfare-dependent and those who seek to help them. I commend it to welfare policymakers and analysts, as well as to teachers, professors, religious leaders, social workers, and all others who are concerned about our citizens and our society.

Preface

In the 1980s, Americans refocused attention on a longstanding and growing problem: the need for reducing welfare dependency. As the culture of poverty evolved into an intractable and often inherited condition for many persons, new ways of encouraging self-sufficiency emerged.

At the federal level, the 1988 passage of the Family Support Act represented a rare show of bipartisan cooperation among Senate, House, and White House. The bill's main thrust was to offer welfare recipients three options: work, job training, or education. Unless they had children age 3 or under, they could no longer get something for nothing; now a return was expected. To smooth the transition from dependency, day care and family eligibility for Medicaid would be continued during the first year of employment. Those choosing job training or education would also be eligible for continued welfare benefits during their study or training period.

At the state level, with federal encouragement, there was a new emphasis on innovation and experimentation. Massachusetts won early acclaim with its ET (Employment and Training) program. Later, California learned from ET's successes and failures in creating GAIN (Greater Avenues for INdependence). Other states such as Wisconsin and Ohio also experimented with new approaches.

Finally, a wide range of local programs, from small employment-training projects that emphasize one-to-one client-counselor relations to comprehensive neighborhood revitalization programs that include employment opportunities, held out new hope for at least some sectors of the welfare-dependent.

These local initiatives were in President-to-be George Bush's mind when he said, "This is America, a nation of communities, of thousands and tens of thousands of ethnic, religious, social, business, labor union, neighborhood, regional, and other organizations . . . a brilliant diversity spread like stars, like a thousand points of light in a broad and peaceful sky." The essays in this anthology survey a variety of programs designed to reduce welfare dependency. They reflect the spirit of innovation, enterprise, and pragmatism of the 1980s as well as the ferment in the debate about welfare policy.

The collection opens with some historical background. Professor Gertrude Himmelfarb examines the early development of British welfare policy, including the famous "New Poor Law" of 1834. Columnist William Raspberry follows with a look at how a well-known nineteenth-century visitor, Alexis de Tocqueville, viewed public welfare in America. Journalist Nicholas Lemann traces the evolution of today's underclass; its poverty is radically different from that of earlier generations, he says, and a major national effort to bring members of this self-destructive culture into the mainstream of society is required.

Picking up where Lemann leaves off, Mickey Kaus proposes the enforcement of a work ethic that would "embody the social norms . . . in danger of disappearing in the underclass culture." There would be no cash welfare for the able-bodied; anyone over eighteen who needed work could get a useful public job and be paid for doing it. The diversity of response to Kaus's proposal in the replies that follow points to a basic theme of this book: that no single approach can deal with the manifold problems of the welfare-dependent, and that multiple short-range and long-range approaches are needed.

Lawrence Mead agrees that the able-bodied should work, though he says that members of the underclass can acquire essential personal habits such as punctuality and dependability through either job training or work. His concern with the impact of welfare dependency on individual character is further explored in Charles Murray's provocative piece, "How Social Policy Affects Behavior."

Complementing (and sometimes contradicting) the experts is Ken Auletta's "The 'Welfare Mentality': Insider Views," in which underclass participants in a New York job-training program discuss their lives and their attitudes toward poverty and society.

In the following two articles, Myron Magnet and the editors of the *Washington Monthly* explore some effective anti-poverty programs. Then, drawing the collection to an optimistic close, businessman Judson Bemis argues that for-profit organizations can deliver some human services effectively and efficiently, and that a combination of public, non-profit, and for-profit resources will give us the best chance of meeting our society's needs.

I am grateful to these authors and their original publishers for permitting us to reprint the articles, in some cases in an abridged form. The statistics and other figures have not been updated. I also want to thank Elizabeth Griffin, a summer 1989 intern at the Ethics and Public Policy Center, who helped with this project. Finally, I owe Carol Griffith, senior editor of the Center, a debt of gratitude both for her judicious and polished editing and for her unflagging spirit of collaboration.

Enormous tasks remain for anyone wishing to help welfare recipients become self-sufficient, productive participants in society. The means to that end examined in the pages that follow are merely a beginning. This volume will have achieved its purpose if it contributes to a better understanding of private alternatives to welfare, and stimulates readers to think and act more imaginatively in the struggle to draw the marginalized among us into the mainstream of society.

TAMAR ANN MEHURON
Research Associate

Ethics and Public Policy Center
Washington, D.C.
April 12, 1990

1

Moral Responsibility: The British Experience

Gertrude Himmelfarb

The English in the late eighteenth and early nineteenth century knew something about the economics of poverty. They knew less than we know, to be sure, and what they knew lacked the precision of our poverty figures, which are given to us in absolute numbers and percentages down to the last tenth of a percentile. Yet the social reformers and social critics of early industrial England were competent enough themselves when it came to statistics.

The first census was in 1801, and it provided information not only about the size of the population but also about occupation. By the 1830s, statistical societies and journals were providing a good deal of information that later historians have judged to be rather accurate, not only about births and deaths, prices and wages, production and consumption, but also about education, crime, housing, and poor relief.

While those pre-Victorians and early Victorians would have envied the sophistication and precision of our statistics, they would not have been deluded. They would have known that poverty cannot be entirely quantified, that it cannot be entirely defined in

Gertrude Himmelfarb is distinguished professor of history emeritus at the Graduate School, City University of New York. Among the books she has written is *The Idea of Poverty: England in the Early Industrial Age*. This essay is adapted from a paper given at a 1985 Ethics and Public Policy Center conference on poverty and welfare.

terms of dollars and cents, or shillings and pence, and that it has a non-economic dimension, which is to say a moral and social dimension, as well.

This seems hardly a novel message. Yet it is one that many historians are only now beginning to learn and some have not yet learned at all. The great controversy among historians of the early industrial period is between the "optimists" and the "pessimists." The optimists maintain that the standard of living of the working classes improved during this period of early industrialism; the pessimists believe it declined. Recently the optimists have been getting the better of this debate, whereupon the pessimists have retreated to a second line of defense: the argument that, even if it could be proved that the standard of living was *materially* improving, nevertheless the *quality of life* of the working classes was deteriorating.

When I started my book called *The Idea of Poverty*, I assumed I would need to find out how the issue had become so distorted: how, given the hard facts of wages and prices and consumption, the significance of those facts could become so controversial. What I discovered was that the optimists are as mistaken as the pessimists, or perhaps not so much mistaken as irrelevant. Yes, the standard of living for the working classes, at least for *most* of the working classes, was increasing and improving for *most* of the early industrial period. But that was not the main concern of contemporaries. What concerned them was the moral and social condition of the poor.

"Standard of living" was not a common expression among the early Victorians. They spoke of the "condition of the people," or, in the phrase made famous by Carlyle, "the condition-of-England question." That question, Carlyle explained, had to do not so much with wages and prices—the "figures of arithmetic," he said—as with the "condition" and the "deposition" of the poor: their "thoughts, beliefs, and feelings," their sense of what was right and wrong, just and unjust. Such ideas and attitudes were conducive either to a "wholesome composure, frugality, and prosperity," or to an "acrid unrest, recklessness, gin-drinking, and gradual ruin."

This kind of language was habitually used by contemporaries. Carlyle was at this time the hero of both Tories and Radicals, of those who wanted to reform the Poor Law and those who wanted it left intact. He was the oracle for people who disagreed about almost everything except this: that the issue was fundamentally a moral one, and that what was at stake was the "demoralization" and "pauperization"—i.e., decline into utter destitution—of the poor.

The Poor Law Debate

The debate over the Poor Law started toward the end of the eighteenth century and culminated with the passage of the New Poor Law in 1834. The Old Poor Law had been in effect since Elizabethan days. It was the first legal, compulsory, secular, national system of relief ever instituted (national in the sense that it was nationwide though administered locally). The amount of relief that was given, to whom it was given, the way it was given, whether in money or in kind, in or out of the poorhouse—all these things varied enormously from time to time and from one part of England to another. But the principle of poor relief was a constant.

By the late eighteenth century, as a result of a variety of circumstances—a series of very poor harvests, high prices, and the dislocations associated with the Napoleonic wars—both the number of people on relief and the cost of relief vastly increased. In part this rise in both numbers and cost reflected the adoption toward the end of the century of what was called the "Speenhamland System," which provided that relief could be given "in aid of wages," that is, as a supplement to the wages of agricultural laborers. The amount of this supplementary relief was determined by the price of bread and the size of the laborer's family.

At this time as much as one-sixth of the population was on relief, and the Poor Law came under intense criticism. The critics charged that the system of relief was hurting rather than helping the poor because it tended to demoralize and pauperize them. To be sure, the reformers were also troubled by the increase in the "poor rates," the local taxes levied for relief. But they were more concerned with the negative effect the system of relief had on the poor themselves, because of its "indiscriminate" nature.

The New Poor Law of 1834 was designed to correct this flaw, to introduce "discriminations" and distinctions. The Royal Commission whose report was the basis of the new law made a large point of distinguishing between "paupers" and "poor," between the laboring poor and indigents, the able-bodied and the infirm.

The Workhouse Principle

The most famous provision of the New Poor Law was the workhouse clause, according to which able-bodied paupers would be taken care of only within the workhouse rather than through "outdoor relief" (the dole). This provision offered a means of determining who was a "pauper" and thus eligible for relief: any able-bodied man who applied for relief knowing that he would receive it only within the confines of the workhouse automatically identified himself as a pauper. The magistrate did not have to inquire into the person's eligibility for relief; the very fact that he sought it under those onerous conditions meant that he was eligible for it. And the workhouse, having defined the pauper, also separated him—physically—from the working poor, thus preventing him from "infecting" them. Within the workhouse there were to be similar distinctions: the able-bodied were to be separated from the sick, males from females, the aged from the young, and so on.

This policy of separation, segregation, differentiation, was also part of the strategy of deterrence. The able-bodied would be loath to apply for relief, not only because conditions in the workhouse would be worse than those of the laborers outside, but also because they would be separated from the rest of the poor. Separation was regarded as a stigma that would serve as the supreme deterrent. It would keep the laborer independent by discouraging him from seeking relief and becoming a pauper. All this would be accomplished while the primary humanitarian purpose of the Poor Law— to provide for those who were either unable or unwilling to provide for themselves—was being fulfilled.

In practice, the workhouse principle was not carried out nearly as systematically as had been proposed. There was far too much resistance to it, not only by the poor but also by the magistrates who had to enforce this provision. As a practical solution, then, the workhouse was a failure. But in another respect it was remarkably successful, for it defined the problem of poverty for that generation and for generations to come. It set the terms of discourse, creating distinctions, definitions, and categories that became part of the mode of thought for the rest of the century—and to a certain extent well beyond that. Ideologically and psychologically, the New Poor Law was almost as important as Puritanism in establishing the ethos that governed social thought and social policy during this critical period of English history. The New Poor Law reinforced and confirmed what we now call the work ethic.

There were, to be sure, important changes in the course of the nineteenth century, especially towards the end, but all of them retained distinctions that were consciously, explicitly moral. They were all based on common assumptions: that the overriding aim of reform was to develop good character; that dependence, even the temptation to dependence, was an invitation to bad character; that work, frugality, temperance, thrift, responsibility, and "respectability" were not bourgeois virtues, as some recent historians like to think, but virtues available to the poor and, under the right conditions and given the proper encouragement, desired by the poor.

The Social Insurance Principle

The first serious challenge to this ethos came with the principle of social insurance. It is fascinating to read the debate between Winston Churchill and Beatrice Webb on the subject of the National Insurance Act of 1911—not a formal debate but one that can be reconstructed from the speeches, letters, and memoirs of the times. Churchill argued in favor of the act on the grounds that the growing complexity of civilization and industrialization required the state to assume responsibility for sickness and unemployment, and that social insurance, far from diminishing the incentives to work and save, would in fact increase those incentives by giving people hope for the future rather than fear. Beatrice Webb, the socialist, opposed the act. She saw social insurance as a "mechanical" way of giving people money without securing from them an advance in conduct. "I fear," she wrote, "the growth of malingering and the right to money independently of the obligation to good conduct."

In retrospect, watching the development first of the "social service state," as it was called, then of the "social security state," then of the "welfare state," and finally, in America, of the "great society," one can see that the principle of social insurance—obligatory no-fault insurance—was a decisive turning point. It marked the beginning of the shift from a philosophy of individual moral responsibility to a philosophy of public, state, or societal responsibility. There is, however, a vast difference between the social-insurance measures adopted before the First World War and the welfare state instituted after the Second World War. The earlier legislation was designed to respond to the most grievous causes of poverty—old age, unemployment, sickness; the later legislation was designed, in effect, to redistribute income.

The idea of social insurance opened the door to the welfare state. Having said that, however, I must add that even in hindsight I cannot resist the arguments in favor of social insurance (the arguments Churchill used at the time), and that I find it difficult to point out where on that slippery slope we should have pulled up short, at what point we should have tried to reassert the principle of personal moral responsibility.

Our problem today is far more difficult than that which the Victorians confronted. Whatever differences the Victorians had, they had the great advantage of operating within a moral consensus, a consensus both about specific moral values and about the centrality of morality in society and in social policy. Today we have no such consensus. We are told that one person's values are as good as another's, and that society cannot presume to impose any set values on its members, not even upon those who are totally dependent upon it for their very subsistence. Yet at the same time we are told that society has an obligation to solve the most refractory moral problems.

Private Charity as Degrading

During a post-graduate seminar for professors that I recently conducted, we were discussing a little-known essay by Tocqueville called "A Memoir on Pauperism." Everyone in the group was enormously impressed by Tocqueville's prescience in anticipating theories that later sociologists would laboriously develop, theories about "relative deprivation," "rising expectations," and "unanticipated consequences." But they were also troubled by Tocqueville's insistence upon the degrading effects of any system of relief given by the state as a matter of right ("entitlement," as we now say). What was really degrading, these professors argued, was not public relief but private charity—voluntary assistance or contributions by friends, neighbors, and relatives.

After they had gone on about this for a while, I asked them whether they thought it was more demeaning for an aged parent to get help from his offspring or to get relief from the state. Their answer was instant and unanimous: it was more demeaning for a parent to be helped by his family than by the state. I asked them to consider the implications of this position. What does it mean about the nature of the family, the relations of parents and children, the sense of personal and familial responsibility, obligation, and duty? How does it affect our ideas of helpfulness, kindness, even love? Although they were troubled by these questions, they could not overcome their instinctive conviction that it was more demeaning to be beholden to one's relatives, one's children, even to one's parents, than to the state.

These, I remind you, were not callow youngsters or graduate students. They were teachers and parents, who themselves were able to recall the attitudes of their own parents during the depression, who would have been deeply ashamed to "go on relief"— who indeed felt about relief much as Victorians felt about the workhouse.

It seems to me that this change of attitude is a primary symptom—perhaps the central feature—of the moral revolution we are now confronting.

2

Tocqueville on Public Welfare

William Raspberry

Perhaps the toughest social problem facing America today is the persistence and growth of the so-called underclass in our affluent society. We don't know how to solve it, and we still debate its causes: alienation, racism, official meanness, isolation, joblessness, loss of moral compass.

I have just seen, in an old issue of *The Public Interest*, an obscure paper of Alexis de Tocqueville suggesting that the debate is a good deal older and more universal than I had thought. Tocqueville, looking at the Europe of 150 years ago, found himself intrigued by a curious phenomenon: the more industrially advanced, the more progressive, the more "civilized" the society, the greater the incidence of pauperism.

Tocqueville was particularly fascinated by England, which in 1835, when he delivered his "Memoir on Pauperism," was the most advanced country in Europe. For all the wealth and graciousness of living that caught the Frenchman's eye, he was struck by something else: one-sixth of the population lived on the public dole. In Spain and Portugal, poorer and less cultivated by far than England, only between 1 and 4 per cent of the inhabitants were indigent.

What lay behind this striking paradox? Two things, Tocqueville told the Royal Academic Society of Cherbourg. First, the more

William Raspberry is a columnist for the *Washington Post*. This article is adapted from columns that appeared in the *Post* on June 11 and 13, 1986, by permission of the publisher.

9

highly developed a society, the more things there are to want and, subsequently, to "need." Indoor plumbing and central heat, once beyond the dreams of kings, are modern-day necessities whose absence constitutes serious misfortune. In primitive societies, "poverty consists only in not finding enough to eat."

Enter: the State

But according to historian Seymour Drescher of the University of Pittsburgh, who discovered the "Memoir" and translated it for his out-of-print book *Tocqueville and Beaumont on Social Reforms*, Tocqueville had another explanation for the paradoxical association of progress and pauperism: public welfare.

By the time of his observations, charity, which earlier had been the province of the monasteries, had been taken over by the state, with overseers in each parish given the right to tax inhabitants in order to feed the disabled and find work for the able-bodied.

It sounds like an eminently reasonable plan—as reasonable as our own welfare system must have seemed to those who devised it— and it worked out about as poorly as our own. Tocqueville thought he understood why:

> Man, like all socially organized beings, has a natural passion for idleness. There are, however, two incentives to work: the need to live and the desire to improve the conditions of life. Experience has proven that the majority of men can be sufficiently motivated to work only by the first of these incentives. The second is effective only with a small minority. Well, a charitable institution indiscriminately open to all those in need, or a law that gives all the poor a right to public aid, whatever the origin of their poverty, weakens or destroys the first stimulant and leaves only the second intact.
>
> The English peasant, like the Spanish peasant, if he does not feel the deep desire to better the position into which he has been born, and to raise himself out of his misery (a feeble desire that is easily crushed in the majority of men)—the peasant of both countries, I maintain, has no interest in working, or, if he works, has no interest in saving. He therefore remains idle or thoughtlessly squanders the fruits of his labors. . . .
>
> Any measure that establishes legal charity on a permanent basis and gives it an administrative form thereby creates an idle and lazy class, living at the expense of the industrial and working class.

Charles Murray couldn't have said it more harshly: our efforts to alleviate poverty only make it worse.

But since a decent society cannot simply ignore poverty, what is to be done? Tocqueville thought he knew, but he never got around to saying. "The measures by which pauperism may be combatted preventively will be the object of a second work which I hope respectfully to submit next year to the Academic Society of Cherbourg," he said at the end of his "Memoir." According to Professor Drescher, Tocqueville shortly afterward ran for the French chamber of deputies and never wrote a second paper.

He did, however leave some notes hinting at the direction of his thinking, Drescher said. The notes underscore Tocqueville's "almost pathological fear of bureaucracy" and suggest that his preference was for worker organizations, self-help groups, and voluntary associations.

"Mediating Structures"

It may be stretching a point, but the things Tocqueville seems to have had in mind sound very much like what Peter Berger and others have described as "mediating structures," defined as "those institutions standing between the individual in his private life and the large institutions of public life."

Clearly Tocqueville shared their preference for private charity and joint undertakings involving families, neighborhoods, churches, and volunteer associations—not because they are cheaper but because they work as public welfare cannot.

Private charity of the sort that preceded England's turn to state welfare "established valuable ties between the rich and the poor," Tocqueville said. "The deed itself involves the giver in the fate of the one whose poverty he has undertaken to alleviate. . . . A moral tie is established between those two classes whose interests and passions so often conspire to separate them from each other, and although divided by circumstance, they are willingly reconciled."

The present-day theorists who speak of "mediating structures" do not prescribe an end of public aid; neither did Tocqueville. Nor do they merely urge the decentralization of government. As Berger and Richard John Neuhaus put it in their paper "To Empower People":

Decentralization is limited to what can be done *within* governmental structures; we are concerned with the structures that stand *between* government and the individual. Nor, again, are we calling for a devolution of governmental responsibilities that would be tantamount to dismantling the welfare state. We aim rather at rethinking the institutional means by which government exercises its responsibilities. The idea is not to revoke the New Deal but to pursue its vision in ways more compatible with democratic governance.

If the new emphasis on private effort sounds a lot like President Reagan's push for voluntarism (for budgetary reasons), it also sounds very much like what the black leadership is saying more and more these days. Both the civil-rights traditionalists and the new black conservatives have begun to stress that the salvation of the inner-city underclass is up to the black middle class: not because government won't do it, or hasn't the means to do it, but because government can't do it.

Tocqueville, that perceptive observer of nineteenth-century social democracy, might wonder what took us so long.

3

Acculturating the Underclass

Nicholas Lemann

There is an air almost of self-congratulation now about discussions of the underclass: see, we're finally talking about it! Crime is a problem in the ghettos. Out-of-wedlock childbearing has gotten out of control. The days of politely avoiding these uncomfortable subjects are over.

Usually this kind of honesty about a problem leads to change for the better. In the case of the underclass it hasn't so far. The reason is that as perceptions of what's going on in the ghettos now have changed, ideas about how things got so bad and what we might do now have stayed the same. The next step is to make breakthroughs in explanation and prescription of the magnitude of the breakthrough in honesty that has taken place.

The ghettos weren't always as bad as they are now. In the twenties, thirties, forties, and fifties, places like Harlem, Roxbury, and the South Side of Chicago were described as being amazingly lively despite the burdens of racism and poverty. They had churches, clubs, restaurants, families. Obviously only a catastrophe could have made them the empty, hopeless places they are today. What was it?

There are two standard answers, opposite ideologically but both rooted in economics. The conservative one, which prevails today, is that government programs, especially welfare and the War on

Nicholas Lemann is a national correspondent for *The Atlantic*. This article is reprinted by permission from the *Washington Post*, September 8, 1986.

Poverty, created "reverse incentives" that encouraged poor blacks to stay poor and to have children out of wedlock. The liberal answer is that the decline of the ghettos parallels a catastrophic rise in unemployment, not in the country as a whole but in the unskilled, inner-city, blue-collar jobs in which urban blacks have traditionally worked.

Both of these theories are partly true, and they're comfortable in the sense that they permit what's mainly a black problem to be discussed without reference to race. But that's also their flaw: Why haven't the reverse incentives built into government programs worked their evils across the whole spectrum of society? Why have millions of people of all races (mostly blacks, but also Koreans, Vietnamese, and Palestinians) found enough economic opportunity to permit an escape from the same inner cities where millions of others seem trapped forever? It would seem that something more than pure economic rationality has been shaping the ghettos.

Two Black Migrations

What created the ghettos in the first place was a mass migration of blacks from the rural South to the urban North—one of the great grass-roots dramas of American history. From World War I until the mid-1960s, about 6.5 million blacks left the South, moving up along the highways and rail lines to get manual-labor jobs that paid double and triple the southern scale.

For most of this time, nearly all blacks had to live in the traditional ghettos, because of the strict residential segregation that prevailed nearly everywhere in the urban North. This meant that the black middle and working classes controlled the ghettos and set the tone there. But in the late sixties, when opportunities of all kinds suddenly opened up for blacks, the ministers and postal workers and schoolteachers began leaving the ghettos and moving to formerly white working-class neighborhoods.

What followed was a second, and less well known, black migration: out of the ghettos. One reason old ghettos look bombed-out and empty is that they have been depopulated since the mid-sixties, often by more than half. The large, new, black middle class does not live in the ghettos.

The Pre-Sixties Underclass

If the underclass is defined as a group prone to out-of-wedlock childbirth, crime, and low educational achievement, there has been an identifiable black underclass for all of this century. It existed to some extent in the northern cities—W. E. B. DuBois's "The Philadelphia Negro" describes the poorest black class in terms that could be used today—but its other home was in the sharecropper cabins of the rural South.

There, until just twenty years ago, a system not so very far removed from slavery prevailed. Education was first forbidden and then severely truncated by whites; large out-of-wedlock families were common; and an ethic of dependency on "The Man" was intentionally fostered. There were no doubt many products of the system who were like the wonderful family in the film *Sounder*, but the unpleasant truth is that there were also many people debilitated by it (see, for a vivid description of one, Richard Wright's portrait of his father in *Black Boy*).

The rest of black society knew perfectly well about the existence of the underclass, especially as its members drifted off the land and into the cities. It was a sensitive subject for middle-class blacks, who knew that the immense social problems of the black lower class would be held up by whites as the justification for keeping all blacks down. The way it was handled, in the days when almost all blacks had to live in ghettos, was by the middle class's using the church, social-improvement organizations, and general physical proximity to preach to the underclass an ethic of acculturation. As a result the underclass stayed noticeable but small; for example, until the sixties the black out-of-wedlock birth rate was five to ten times the white rate, but it was still low compared with today, between 10 and 20 per cent.

The Post-Sixties Underclass

In the late sixties, when, the statistics show, the underclass quickly became a major problem, there was more than just the War on Poverty and the loss of many unskilled city jobs going on. The leadership, the institutional structure, and indeed most of the working and married population were leaving the underclass alone in the ghettos.

The mass construction of highways and housing projects during this time helped to complete the physical isolation of the underclass. At the same time, a kind of moral isolation was going on, too, because the rest of society became empathetic to the underclass's problems to the point of explaining them away. The kind of preaching to the underclass that had gone on before was now dismissed as an example of "blaming the victim."

It was then that the out-of-wedlock birth rate, the crime rate, and the dropout rate really soared; what sociologists call "social disorganization" had set in. Today, though certainly the people in ghettos are victims in every way imaginable, what distorts their lives most obviously isn't society as a whole but the particular culture in the ghettos, whose rules often dictate such life-dooming activities as out-of-wedlock pregnancy for girls and petty crime for boys.

Here, though, the disagreements over what to do about the ghettos begin. In the rarefied circles in which policy is debated, the word "culture" is still regarded as deeply offensive—a code way of saying that poor blacks occupy an inferior position in society because they are innately, even racially, inferior. William Julius Wilson of the University of Chicago, who has done courageous and pioneering work on the split in black America and the irrelevance of civil-rights legislation to the underclass, flatly told *Washington Post* columnist Dorothy Gilliam recently that there is no such thing as a poverty culture.

At the other end of the ideological spectrum, Charles Murray's *Losing Ground*, which is really a book about the underclass, doesn't discuss culture either.

Three Proposed Solutions

There are currently three leading sets of proposed solutions to the problem of the underclass. First is the venerable liberal cause of full employment, with perhaps targeted help given to industries in the northern cities. Second is cutting welfare, probably in the guise of creating a social-services block grant to be controlled by the state governments. Third is "community development" programs that would, through a kind of mass self-help effort, make the ghettos bloom again.

If culture is a significant part of the problem, none of these will completely solve it; if that seems like a big chance to take, then maybe we should consider culture in discussing what to do next.

Discussing culture need not be an opening for racists. Certainly evil has been done in its name, but on the whole the sense that there is a national culture that is defined not by race but by an idealistic set of principles is something for the country to be proud of. The urge to bring people into the mainstream is, again, a mostly noble one—it was the rhetorical underpinning of the civil-rights movement.

A solution to the problem of the underclass that took culture into account would have to use work as its primary tool, but it wouldn't be limited to lowering the unemployment rate. The process of ending the underclass's segregation from the rest of the country would begin with Head Start–like education projects in earliest childhood and proceed through government-supplied jobs outside the ghettos that would be a transitional step into the real job market, whose health the government would have to safeguard too, of course.

You may think that all of this has been tried before, that government programs don't work, that the problems are too deeply ingrained to be solved. But (1) it hasn't been tried as a major national effort with the clear-eyed goal of acculturation; (2) there was a time when major efforts to use the government to solve national problems *did* work; and (3) many other groups in the past have been considered unassimilable, always wrongly. On race of all issues, where we have seen so much change for the better in a single generation and where there is still a healthy charge of moral righteousness left in us, it would be sad if we stopped now.

4

The Work Ethic State

Mickey Kaus

Poverty in America forms a culture, a way of life and feeling, that makes it a whole."
Who said that? Here's a hint—he wrote in the early 1960s. Here's another: he dramatically portrayed the breakdown of family life in the black ghetto, the tendency of young men to move from one woman to another without forming marital bonds, and the disastrous rise in the number of families headed by women. This new culture, he said, was different from the culture of other poor ethnic immigrants—more isolated, more dispiriting, more self-perpetuating.

Give up? Did you guess Daniel Patrick Moynihan, author of a famous 1965 government report on this topic? Well, you're wrong. If you guessed Kenneth Clark, the black sociologist whose book *Dark Ghetto* anticipated much of Moynihan's report—you're also wrong. The quote is from the socialist Michael Harrington—from his 1962 book *The Other America*, generally credited with prodding a Democratic administration into launching the War on Poverty.

More recently, it was Ronald Reagan who warned of "a permanent culture of poverty . . . a second and separate America." Reagan conservatives blamed the growth of this underclass on the antipoverty war Harrington started. The mere existence of this under-

Mickey Kaus is West Coast correspondent for *The New Republic*. This essay is abridged by permission from an article in the July 7, 1986, issue of that magazine (© 1986, The New Republic, Inc.).

19

class is considered a refutation of liberalism, and many liberals seem to react as if that were true. But as the Harrington quotation shows, we really haven't come very far since 1962, when the War on Poverty hadn't even begun.

In the intervening years, much of America's policy establishment fled from the underclass problem. Black leaders, caught up in the enterprise of building ethnic pride ("black is beautiful") and worried in part that an unflattering description of ghetto life would reflect on all blacks, reacted against Moynihan's report, enforcing an etiquette of silence on the subject. Liberal whites, frustrated by the failure of the "hand-up-not-hand-out" programs of the early Great Society, nevertheless were reluctant to "blame the victim." Instead, they gravitated toward a bland redistributionism which held that if the poor couldn't or wouldn't earn their way out of poverty, the government should simply give them cash in the form of a guaranteed income.

Now we're back at the beginning. There is justified doubt that cash in itself can end the pathology. No one who has watched Bill Moyers's "CBS Reports" on the black family's decline, or read Leon Dash's series on black teenage pregnancy in the *Washington Post*, or Nicholas Lemann's *Atlantic* articles on "The Origins of the Underclass," or Ken Auletta's book on the same subject, can doubt that there is a culture of poverty out there that has taken on a life of its own. Right and left now recognize that neither robust economic growth nor massive government transfer payments can by themselves transform a "community" where 90 per cent of the children are born into fatherless families, where over 60 per cent of the population is on welfare, where the work ethic has evaporated and the entrepreneurial drive is channeled into gangs and drug-pushing.

The underclass embraces only a minority of the poor. It doesn't even include most who go on welfare. On the other hand, about 10 to 15 per cent of single mothers who go on welfare stay there for eight years or more, and they account for about half the money spent on welfare at any one time, according to a study by David Ellwood and Mary Jo Bane of Harvard. These people, who are poor on a more or less permanent basis, are part of whom we're talking about.

Is the underclass black? Certainly it does not include most blacks, two-thirds of whom live above the poverty line. But a large ongoing survey at the University of Michigan shows that although blacks compose only 12 per cent of the population, they make up 62 per cent of those who stay poor for a long time and 58 per cent of the "latent poor"—that is, those who would be poor but for welfare. In this respect the old stereotype that most of the poor are black is accurate.

The statistics are equally striking on the question of family breakup. Black illegitimacy rates have always been many times higher than white rates. Then, starting around 1965, the black rate rose dramatically from its already high Moynihan-report level of 25 per cent to close to 60 per cent today. White illegitimacy rates have been rising, too, but the white rate is still only about 13 per cent.

So yes, the problem I am talking about is the culture of our largely black, largely urban ghettos. It is only part of the broader problem of poverty, although it is the most intractable part. It is only part of the problem facing black Americans, although all blacks are unfairly stigmatized by the behavior of the underclass minority. Today, when most liberal black leaders are finally speaking frankly about the crisis in the ghettos, the important question is no longer whether there *is* a culture of poverty, but what we are going to do to change it.

"Let Blacks Do It"

One possible solution is "self-help," which means efforts by the black middle and upper classes to perform what *Washington Post* columnist William Raspberry has called "an unprecedented and enormously difficult salvage operation" in the ghetto. This strategy accords with both the hesitancy of liberal whites to tell blacks how to behave and the interest of bootstrapping black neoconservatives in shifting the focus away from a "civil rights" strategy that relies on government intervention. "Only blacks can effectively provide moral leadership for their people," says Glenn Loury of Harvard, a prime spokesman for self-help. More successful blacks, especially, are "strategically situated" to undertake this task. Even Loury's liberal black critics, such as Roger Wilkins, accept both the need for changing underclass culture and the assumption that "only black people can do this." Let-Blacks-Do-It is the new left-right consensus.

When you get to just how the black community itself is going to accomplish a "massive cultural turnaround," however, things get vague. Loury talks about "discussion of values" and "building constructive, internal institutions." Wilkins admits he has only "the sketchiest of ideas." The "local Urban League," he says, could "assemble a roster of role models and present them as a package of assembly speakers for inner-city schools."

Good luck to such efforts, but let's be realistic: today's underclass infants will be great-great-grandparents before these well-intentioned and pathetically limited schemes accomplish any "massive cultural turnaround." The "luckier blacks" can't do it themselves. I'm not even sure it's fair to expect middle-class blacks to bear the load of reshaping the underclass simply because they share the same skin color.

Nor is it clear that all the black talk of "self-help"—tinged as it often is with separatism—will push in the right direction. Above all, the Let-Blacks-Do-It boom tempts non-blacks to avoid thinking with any urgency about solutions to the problem that everyone is so proud to have reacknowledged.

The alternative is to search for the sort of sweeping government effort that has helped solve our other problems—not new civil-rights laws, but efforts that might have the same beneficial effect as the early civil-rights laws. As Moynihan says, in the best two sentences in his book *Family and Nation*, "The central conservative truth is that it is culture, not politics, that determines the success of a society. The central liberal truth is that politics can change a culture and save it from itself."

The Bribe Theory

If you're looking for a political handle on the culture of poverty, there is none bigger than welfare.

What is wrong with the current welfare state, anyway? The basic features of our current system for the poor are these: Fairly generous benefits are available to those deemed totally and permanently disabled. Very little in the way of benefits (mainly Food Stamps and stingy state "general relief" money) is available to able-bodied men and women, single or married. But if you are a single parent (almost always a mother) responsible for taking care of a child, you qualify for Aid to Families with Dependent Children (AFDC), which is what most people mean by welfare. In California and New York, the AFDC benefit, combined with other benefits, is high enough to bring a welfare mother close to the poverty line. In most Southern states the AFDC benefit is much lower.

The central dilemma of our welfare state, then, is not the age-old general tension between "compassion" and "dependency." For most of the able-bodied, Americans have decided against much cash compassion. Ours is a more specific and modern dilemma: what about a single able-bodied woman who must also care for a child? If we give her no more aid than we give able-bodied men, we may be punishing the child. But to aid the child, we must aid the mother, as AFDC does—and then we risk the "social hazard" of encouraging women to put themselves in that disastrous position. To women, the AFDC system seems to say, "Have a child and the state will take care of you—as long as you don't live with the father." To men, it says, "Father children and the state will take care of them."

This can't *help*. But the conservative attack on welfare mixes up two quite distinct theories as to how it might *hurt*. According to theory one, prospective mothers and fathers are influenced directly by the economic blandishments of AFDC, much as if by bribes. A mother might have a baby "to go on welfare." A father might leave his wife or girlfriend so that she qualifies for the program. Believers in this theory are apt to say that welfare *caused* the growth of the underclass.

The Umbilical Cord Theory

But there is a second, and far more plausible, theory that implicates welfare in this cultural catastrophe. It holds that although welfare might not *cause* the underclass, it *sustains* it. With AFDC in place, young girls look around them and recognize, perhaps unconsciously, that girls in their neighborhood who have had babies on their own are surviving, however uncomfortably (but who lives comfortably in the ghetto?). Welfare, as the umbilical cord through which the mainstream society sustains the isolated ghetto society, permits the expansion of this single-parent culture.

The Umbilical Cord Theory doesn't talk of families being directly "pulled apart" by welfare, but of families that are never formed in the culture that welfare subsidizes. Once AFDC benefits reach a certain threshold that allows poor single mothers to survive, the culture of the underclass can start growing as women have babies for all the various non-welfare reasons they have them. Indeed, precisely because nobody has babies in order to go on welfare, marginally lowering welfare benefits won't affect them.

The Umbilical Cord Theory underlies Charles Murray's notorious "thought experiment." What would happen, he asks, if there were no welfare *at all*? Answer: things would have to change. "You want to cut illegitimate births among poor people? . . . I know how to do that," Murray told Ken Auletta in a *Washington Monthly* interview. "You just rip away every kind of government support there is. What happens then? You're going to have lots of parents talking differently to daughters, and you're going to have lots of daughters talking differently to their boyfriends." If the daughters didn't, their plight trying to raise kids without welfare would serve as an example to their neighbors.

The implications of this second view of welfare are far nastier than those of the Bribe version. If the Umbilical Cord Theory is correct, it isn't enough to *extend* welfare benefits so that intact families are well off in comparison to single-parent families. You have to deny benefits to the single-parent families, to unplug the underclass culture's life-support system.

The "Workfare" Option

Those of us who don't have the stomach to go through with Murray's "experiment" (and Murray himself waffles) are compelled to come up with a more humane way of changing the welfare culture. And there remains the possibility that something less than Murray's "let them starve" solution might work—something that doesn't cause pain exactly, but that does impose upon individuals the consequences of their choices, at the same time that it offers them a way out.

This is the promise of "workfare," which in the late 1980s is the hottest thing in the hot field of welfare reform. Workfare holds out the hope of achieving the ends of Murray's "experiment" without the intolerable toll of human suffering, simply by exposing welfare recipients to the necessity that has been the fate of mankind since Eden: the necessity of labor.

In 1969, when Nixon proposed his ambitious guaranteed-income scheme for families with children, his domestic advisor, one Daniel Patrick Moynihan, threw in a token "work requirement" to placate conservatives. This gave William Safire, Nixon's speechwriter, the excuse he needed to label the entire concoction "workfare," thus permanently confusing the meaning of that term. The Nixon plan, in reality, offered the poor money with no strings attached. As such it was the opposite of what I mean by workfare, which is what Ronald Reagan meant when he first proposed in 1967 that welfare recipients in California be required to work, in government public-service jobs if necessary, in exchange for their welfare checks.

Workfare drove liberals berserk back then. Thanks in part to liberal opposition, Reagan's California program never got off the ground. But he persisted, and when he got to Washington in 1981 he proposed requiring all states to make welfare recipients work off their grants at the minimum wage. Congress didn't give him that, but it did allow states to experiment with workfare if they wanted.

The result is one of those bipartisan movements that seem to herald a genuinely productive marriage of liberalism with the more authoritarian wing of conservatism. At least twenty-eight states have run experiments, most of them small, with one or another variety of workfare.

The appearance of a new bipartisan toughness can be deceiving, however. Virtually everybody by now agrees that welfare recipients, mothers included, should be in the labor force. Beyond that, "workfare"—like "industrial policy"—is vague enough to mean quite different things to different people.

ET in Massachusetts

On one extreme is Massachusetts's touted Employment and Training Choices program, ET for short. But ET is not really workfare at all. There is nothing mandatory about it. True, welfare mothers with no children under six must *register* for the program, but registration for work has been a federal welfare requirement since 1967. Everything else about ET is voluntary. Welfare mothers are offered a variety of services designed to help find them work—job appraisals, career-planning workshops, remedial education, job training, placement services. Those who find jobs get transportation allowances and free day care for a year after they start work, plus Medicaid for up to fifteen months if their employers don't provide health insurance.

But welfare recipients don't have to do any of this. If they prefer they can still stay home and collect a check.

Why might ET make a difference where similar programs failed? First, it seems to have changed the perception that welfare mothers are unemployable. Various studies have shown that, of all "underclass" groups, AFDC mothers are the most capable of making the transition to the world of work. (It's the men who are most often unemployable.)

Second, there are undoubted advantages to ET's all-carrot, Up With People approach. "If we went confrontational, they would feel criticized, scared, angry," argues Anne Peretz, director of the Family Center, a clinic that serves welfare recipients living in public housing. "You can get everybody up and marching in the right direction, but you will lose the war" unless the behavior is truly self-motivated. Peretz sees no alternative to coaxing and cajoling welfare cases into action by appealing to "that part of themselves" that wants to become self-supporting, a process she likens to "seduction."

But ET doesn't come close to "solving the problem" of the culture of poverty. ET is about as good a voluntary job-training program as we are likely to get. It is competently run, well funded, skillfully marketed. It operates in what has been the hottest regional economy in the country. But of 112,983 welfare cases in 1985, about 7,660, or 6.8 per cent, actually got full-time jobs through ET. Even if all those people wouldn't have found work otherwise, that isn't a big enough percentage to transform the underclass. Those remaining are the least motivated, the hardest to "seduce." ET offers those willing to work their way out of the culture of poverty a way to do it, no small thing. But it leaves the culture itself largely unscathed.

GAIN in California

The problem is that there are people who won't climb up a "ladder of opportunity" even when the economy or the government dangles it in front of their noses. If it's dramatic change we want, we must look to programs that "make" people do things they might not do if they have had a check coming every month. I say "make" with caution, given the liberty with which terms like "slavery" are used in the workfare debate. Nobody is talking about throwing indigents in jail if they don't work. True workfare—the mandatory kind—merely says that if you take the state's money, the state has a right to ask something in return.

If George Deukmejian, California's Republican governor, could talk like Mario Cuomo, we would all have heard more than enough about GAIN (Greater Avenues for INdependence), the welfare-reform plan that sailed through his state's legislature early in 1986. But Deukmejian is a bore, so the most important welfare reform in decades went largely unnoticed in the Eastern press.

GAIN is big. It tries to impose a mandatory program on the largest welfare caseload in the country. Unlike ET, under GAIN recipients must do *something*. No welfare recipient will be forced to work off her grant right away. If she doesn't get a job after training in a specific job skill, then the state may require her to work off her grant—but it must offer her a workfare job that uses the skill she has learned. Welfare mothers trained as nurses' aides may not be required to work as secretaries. Only if the recipient screws up in some way—drops out of school or falls out of the training program—may she be required to take a long-term public-service job unrelated to her training. These "long-term PREP" ("pre-employment preparation") cases are reviewed every six months, and may then be recycled through the system.

As a hard workfare strategy to destroy the poverty culture, GAIN suffers from the two major structural flaws common to most such programs. First, it requires nothing of welfare mothers until their youngest child reaches the age of six. This one restriction excuses two-thirds of the welfare caseload in California.

Even more important, neither GAIN nor any mere "workfare" plan does much to employ those in the underclass who have few welfare benefits to "work off," namely able-bodied men. A welfare mother whose ET session I observed asked if there were any way the program could find a job for her "friend." That was the third such request the caseworker had had that day. It will be hard to break the culture of single motherhood as long as among non-whites aged 20–24 there are only 48 employed civilian—i.e., "marriageable"—men for every 100 women (as William Julius Wilson and Kathryn Neckerman of the University of Chicago estimate). In fact, the absolute number of illegitimate black births has not been increasing, but the rate at which legitimate black families are formed has plummeted.

No program is apt to arrest this decline unless it puts more men into jobs. By offering women who head fatherless families a way out of poverty, while failing to offer it to potential fathers (or childless women), work and training programs may reinforce whatever incentives in favor of single-parent families the AFDC system generates.

Only Work Works

What would a program that had a real chance of undermining the underclass look like? The deficiencies in the efforts currently under way give us some idea. First, it would expect women to work even if they have young children. Second, it would offer work to ghetto men and single women as well as to the welfare mothers. Third, it would deal with two related dilemmas: (1) How can you require welfare recipients to accept private jobs if they pay less than welfare? (2) How can you avoid making workfare or training more lucrative than private-sector work?

Solving these problems will take something more radical than any existing workfare plan. It must be far bigger, in order to offer jobs to men, and far tougher in its dealings with young mothers. Above all, the program must unambiguously announce the cultural norm it seeks to promote in place of the culture of welfare.

What is required, I think, is something like this: replacing all cash-like welfare programs that assist the *able-bodied* poor (AFDC, general relief, Food Stamps, and housing subsidies, but not Medicaid) with a single, simple offer from the government—an offer of employment for every American citizen over eighteen who wants it, in a useful public job at a wage slightly below the minimum wage. If you could work, and needed money, you would not be given a check (welfare). You would not be given a check and then cajoled, instructed, and threatened into working it off or "training it off" (workfare). You would be given the location of several government job sites. If you showed up, and worked, you would be paid for your work. If you didn't show up, you would not get paid. Simple.

Unlike "workfare" jobs, these jobs would be available to everybody, men as well as women, single or married, mothers and fathers alike. No perverse "anti-family" incentives. No "means test" either. If David Rockefeller showed up, he could work, too. But he wouldn't. Most Americans wouldn't. The low wage itself would "ration" the jobs to those who needed them most, and preserve the incentive to look for better work in the private sector. Instead of paying what in effect are high workfare "wages" and then relying on the stigma of welfare to encourage people to leave, this program would pay low wages but remove the stigma. Those who worked in the jobs would be earning their money. They could hold their heads up. They would also have something most unemployed underclass members desperately need: a supervisor they could give as a job reference to other employers. Although the best workers could be promoted to higher-paying public-service positions, for most workers movement into the private sector would take care of itself. If you have to work anyway, why do it for $3 an hour?

Those who didn't take advantage of these jobs, however, would be on their own. No cash doles, mothers included. (Remember, we're talking here only about those *able* to work.) A worker who showed up drunk or high, or who picked a fight with his or her supervisor, could be fired (though he or she could show up again after a decent interval). There would be no need to "require" work; work would be all that was offered. The problem of having to take away high benefits to force low-wage work would be solved by simply not providing those benefits in the first place.

The Work Ethic State

This is not a new idea. Similar proposals have been advanced in the past by Russell Long and (of all people) Arthur Burns. Basically, it makes the same decision Franklin Roosevelt made in 1934, when he decided to replace a system of cash relief for the able-bodied with the Work Projects Administration, the WPA. Liberals who invoke Roosevelt's "compassionate" legacy tend to forget this anti-dole decision, while conservatives who quote Roosevelt's description of the dole as "a narcotic" somehow fail to mention that the words were said in the speech where FDR proposed the largest government jobs program in the nation's history.

Of course, Roosevelt's WPA was designed to combat general unemployment at a time when most of those needing "relief" were veteran workers. Nobody imagined that the tiny AFDC program, nestled unnoticed in the New Deal structure, would one day sustain millions of husbandless mothers. Our goal, in contrast, is to break the culture of poverty by providing jobs for ghetto men and women who may have no prior work habits, at the same time as we end the option of a life on welfare for single mothers. It is the transformation of the welfare state into the Work Ethic State, in which status, dignity, and government benefits flow only to those who work, but in which the government steps in to make sure work is available to all.

There are a number of obvious objections to so simple a solution:

Will the wage be enough to support a family? No. The poverty line for a family of three in 1986 was $8,570. A full-time, minimum-wage job brought in only $7,000, and the government jobs proposed here would pay less than that. But there are ways to supplement the incomes of low-wage workers while preserving an incentive to seek better pay. The current Earned Income Tax Credit is one; another is the innovative Wage Rate Subsidy system of Brandeis professor Robert Lerman, which would pay half the difference between the family breadwinner's wage and $6 an hour. Even Ronald Reagan once proposed this approach while testifying against the guaranteed income in 1972.

A subsidized wage would, in effect, be a guaranteed income *for those who work*, a far more affordable proposition than an income guarantee that doesn't start from a base of wages. There is no objection, in the Work Ethic State, to the government's sending out checks as long as able-bodied people get them only if they work. Supplementing wages is a much better solution to the Low Wage problem than pretending the underclass can get "good jobs" that pay enough in themselves to support a family.

Will people be allowed to starve? The state's basic obligation, in this scheme, is to provide dignified work for those who can work, and a decent income for the disabled. There will be those who refuse to work. Many ghetto men, at least initially, will prefer the world of crime, hustle, and odd jobs to working for "chump change." One advantage of the Work Ethic State is that criminals can be treated as criminals, without residual guilt about the availability of jobs. Others—the addled and the addicted—will simply fail at working, or not even try. Even a fraction of welfare mothers, the most employable underclass group, will have trouble. "The workplace is so foreign to so many people who are second- and third-generation dependents," says Tom Nees, a Washington, D.C., minister whose Community of Hope works with welfare families poor enough to be homeless.

The first underclass generation *off* welfare will be the roughest. Those people who fail at work will be thrown into the world of austere public in-kind guarantees—homeless shelters, soup kitchens, and the like—and the world of private charitable organizations like Nees's. This aid would be stigmatizing (as it must be if work is to be honored), but it could be compassionate. Nobody would starve. Counseling, therapy, training, could be offered, even subsidized by the government, in order to help these people back on their feet. The one thing the government would not offer them is cash.

What about mothers with young children? The government would announce that, after a certain date, single mothers would no longer qualify for cash welfare payments. The central ambiguity of our welfare system—whether single mothers should work—would be resolved cleanly in favor of work. This hard choice is a key way the Work Ethic State would hope to break the self-perpetuating culture of poor, single-parent families. Teenage mothers who had babies could no longer count on welfare to sustain them. They would have to work like everyone else, and the prospect of juggling mother-hood and a not very lucrative job would make them think twice, although it would also offer a way out of poverty that Charles Murray's starvation solution would deny.

What would the children do when their mothers were working? If the government is going to expect poor mothers to work, then it will have to provide day care for all who need it. This will be expensive (Massachusetts pays $2,800 a year for each day-care slot). But it won't be as prohibitively expensive as many who raise the day-care issue seem to believe. In every state in which free day care has been offered to AFDC mothers, demand has fallen below predictions. "It is never utilized to the extent people thought it would be," says Barbara Goldman of Manpower Demonstration Research Corporation, which has done studies of workfare programs. Most mothers, it seems, prefer to make their own arrangements. Whether those arrangements are any good is another question. The government might actually have to take steps to encourage day care, as part of the general trend toward getting kids out of underclass families and into school at an early age.

What about mothers with very young children? A destitute mother with a newborn infant presents the basic AFDC dilemma in its starkest form. It *is* a dilemma, meaning there are arguments on both sides. One alternative is to allow temporary cash welfare for the first two years of a child's life, with a three-year limit to avoid the have-another-kid loophole. A two-year free ride is better than a six-year free ride. Teenagers are likely to be friends with someone in their community who has a two-year-old child and is "up against it," as Murray puts it. On the other hand, no free ride at all (except for in-kind nutritional assistance during pregnancy and infancy to avoid disastrous health problems) would clearly have stronger impact. It would also put mothers into the world of work without letting them grow accustomed to dependency. Oklahoma applies its fairly "soft" workfare requirement to mothers as soon as their babies are born, with no apparent ill effects.

And if a mother refuses? The short, nasty answer is that if a mother turns down the state's offer of a job with which she might support her children, and as a result her children live in squalor and filth, then she has neglected a basic task of parenthood. She is subject to the laws that already provide for removal of a child from an unfit home.

What about teenagers who haven't finished high school? They could receive free day care while finishing, and in-kind nutritional assistance, but no cash. To obtain any extra cash necessary to support a baby, they would have to work, in one of the guaranteed government jobs if necessary. Again, the government could offer as many free training programs as it wanted, but without cash entitlements. Since training would no longer be an alternative to working, trainees would have every incentive to make the most of it.

Will there be enough jobs these people can do? The objection can't be that there are not enough worthwhile jobs to be done. The crumbling "infrastructure" that preoccupied Washington in the recent past hasn't been patched up overnight. All around the country governments have stopped doing, for financial reasons, things they once thought worthwhile, like opening libraries on Saturday and picking up trash twice a week. Why not do them again?

The Suitability Question

There are plausible doubts about whether the welfare recipients who need such jobs would be suited to doing them. One objection concerns women and physical labor: Are we really going to have teenage girls repairing potholes and painting bridges? Why not? Women can fill potholes and paint bridges (and water lawns and pick up garbage), just as women can be telephone repairmen and sailors. Feminism has rightly destroyed the sex stereotypes that used to surround much physical work. Anyway, there are many non-arduous "women's" jobs that need doing—nurses' aides, Xerox operators, receptionists, clerks, coat checkers, cooks, and cleaners. Private schools often require parents to keep order on playgrounds twice a month. Public schools might employ one or two parents to do the same full-time. Day-care centers could, too.

Is there any point in offering women free day care and then putting some of them to work in day-care centers? Yes. First, that would still free up a lot of women for employment. Second, and more important, the day-care jobs would exist within the culture of work—with alarm clocks to set, appointments to keep, and bosses to please—rather than the culture of welfare.

A second objection has to do with competence. Can an illiterate, immature high school dropout be trusted to work in a hospital as a nurses' aide, or in a public office as a clerk? Maybe not. But who can't sweep a floor? The liberals who make this objection often seem to have an opinion of underclass capability that makes William Shockley look generous. In fact, supervisors of soft-workfare workers polled by the MDRC rated welfare recipients as productive as regular entry-level workers. For those with severe limitations—well, even raking leaves is a useful service. If that is all someone is capable of doing, does that mean she should not be paid for doing it? The alternative, remember, is to pay her to stay home and raise children.

A third objection is that any program will inevitably degenerate into makework. Exhibit A here is not the WPA, which left a whole legacy of valuable public works. The problem is CETA, the Ford-Carter program that is now universally condemned as a boondoggle. CETA (Comprehensive Employment and Training Act) was a disaster for a variety of reasons, but one big reason was that doing anything useful would have offended unions. Construction unions insisted on restrictions that basically precluded CETA from building anything. AFSCME (American Federation of State, County and Municipal Employees) was on guard lest CETA provide any useful service that might be performed by civil servants. So we had CETA workers in experimental film workshops and mime troupes. In California they took a dog and cat census.

It's not as if government unions are wrong to think a guaranteed job program will hurt them. It will. But at some point, if we are serious about breaking the poverty culture, we must be serious enough to sacrifice the interests of the protected group. Why should well-paid government workers be shielded from the competitive labor market at the expense of the poorest segment of society?

Pragmatism, if not fairness, requires that no current government workers be laid off. As those workers leave through natural attrition, however, the government would be free to replace them with guaranteed jobholders. Guaranteed job projects could then be chosen on the basis of how useful they are, not whether the union objects to them. Wherever possible, they would be designed to produce a tangible benefit—collected garbage, a clean subway station, a basketball hoop with a new net—that the public could see. If they took underclass workers outside the ghetto, so much the better. Projects could be ongoing, expanding as necessary in times of high unemployment. Vague-sounding service efforts— drop-in centers for veterans, community organizing—would be avoided, not because they aren't valuable, but because results are hard to measure and the possibility of spending all day doing very little is high.

Yes, public-works jobs would be relatively inefficient compared with their private-sector counterparts. The government would have to learn to work with the dregs of the labor market, and the program (like the most successful War on Poverty program, the Job Corps) would have to be relatively authoritarian. Boondoggles would happen. But at least the public would be getting *something* for its money.

Won't it cost a fortune? The WPA, at its peak, employed 3.3 million people full time. CETA, at its peak, employed 750,000. At the pit of the last recession, there were 11.4 million unemployed (4.6 million for more than fifteen weeks). What fraction of them would want sub-minimum-wage jobs—and how many of those not in the labor force would come out of the woodwork to claim those jobs—is anybody's guess. It's usually more expensive, at least initially, to give people jobs than to give them cash welfare. Jobs require materials and expensive supervisors. A reasonable estimate, based on previous programs, is about $10,000 per job. That's $10 billion for every million jobs. Pretty soon you're talking real money.

The long-run savings, of course, would be huge if the welfare culture was absorbed into the working, tax-paying culture. In the short run, however, welfare savings would be less, and the benefit of the work done would show up as savings only if it was work the government would be doing anyway.

Would these short-term savings balance out the extra short-term costs? Probably not. Who cares? The point is not to save money. The point is to enforce the work ethic. This is a long-term cultural offensive, not a budget-control program or an expression of compassion. The sharpness and simplicity of its choices—no cash welfare for the able-bodied, no exceptions for parenthood—are its main virtue because they embody with unmistakable clarity the social norms that are in danger of disappearing in the underclass culture.

In sum: Welfare does not work. Work "incentives" do not work. Training does not work. Work "requirements" do not work. "Work experience" does not work, and even workfare does not quite work. Only work works.

"The Work Ethic State": Responses

Mickey Kaus's article "The Work Ethic State" seems to have crystallized an emerging and overdue national debate about the poor in America. Kaus proposed scrapping the current welfare system completely and replacing it with a guaranteed WPA-style public-service jobs program. But Kaus's plan had several unusual twists. First, he called for making work mandatory. Employable poor people who refused to take a job would receive no public assistance. Second, he proposed that these jobs pay less than the current minimum wage so as to keep them from siphoning off workers currently employed in the private sector.

We asked several experts for their reaction to Kaus's article and for their own thoughts on how America can reduce the numbers of people living in poverty.

Barbara Ehrenreich and Frances Fox Piven are collaborating on a book responding to right-wing positions on social welfare issues. **Robert Kuttner**, the *New Republic*'s economics correspondent, defended the European-style welfare state in his book *Economic Illusion*. **Sylvia Ann Hewlett**, an economist and the author of *A Lesser Life: The Myth of Women's Liberation in America*, is a member of the Project on the Welfare of Families, co-chaired by Arizona governor Bruce Babbitt and Arthur S. Fleming. **William Julius Wilson**, professor of sociology at the University of Chicago, is best known for his work arguing that the significance of race in American society is declining while class differences are becoming more pronounced. **David T. Ellwood** is associate professor of public policy at Harvard's Kennedy School of Government. His studies with Mary Jo Bane have shown that higher welfare benefits don't seem to encourage the breakup of families. **Lawrence Mead**, associate professor of politics at New York University, argues in his book *Beyond Entitlement* that the welfare system has failed because it is too permissive. **Charles Murray** staked out the definitive

Reprinted by permission from the October 6, 1986, issue of *The New Republic*.

conservative critique of Great Society social programs of the 1960s in *Losing Ground*, where he contended that the welfare system has created a dependent class.—THE EDITORS, *The New Republic*.

1. THE ALARM CLOCK SYNDROME

Barbara Ehrenreich and Frances Fox Piven

Mickey Kaus proposes to abolish the "culture of poverty," which according to his estimate flourishes among 10 to 15 per cent of welfare recipients, by abolishing welfare. This is analogous to closing all hospitals because some people get sick in them, or abolishing the postal service because a tiny minority uses it to perpetrate fraud. We do not question whether Kaus's proposal will work; you can always kill a fly with a hand grenade. What about the other 85 to 90 per cent of single mothers on welfare who would be herded up, along with the presumed degenerates, into morally uplifting public-sector jobs paying three dollars an hour? Many of these are recent divorcees, often from middle-class marriages, who need welfare while they regroup, find child care, and attempt to enter the job market. Some are wives in flight from abusive husbands, temporarily homeless and traumatized. Most are already victims of a job market that specializes in offering women work that is episodic or part-time and that pays far less than the penurious "poverty level" calculated by the federal government. These women, who somehow manage to raise their children singlehandedly *and* piece together a living on Burger King–level jobs and social welfare crumbs, are—with all due respect to the stressed-out yuppies of media fame—among the hardest-working people in America.

But leaving them aside for a minute, let us consider the "dregs of the work force" who are the intended beneficiaries of Kaus's proposal. Suppose that they *are* all wallowing in the "culture of poverty," and suppose that this is indeed a lamentable state—much worse, say, than the "culture of Wall Street." Kaus is not proposing to do anything about their poverty—at least not seriously at three dollars an hour and a wave of the hand to Earned Income Tax

Credits. All he proposes to change is their "culture." The poor will be as poor as ever, but they will know how to wind an alarm clock.

There is another approach, so ancient as to be once again novel: leave the "culture" of the poor alone for the moment and try to do something about their *poverty*. For example, raise AFDC (welfare) benefits to an amount that a family could decently live on—say, the median family income (about $27,000 a year) or even half of that. Too expensive? Remember, "the point isn't to save money," as Kaus tells us, it's to abolish the underclass. As the squalor of poverty lifts—and with it the awful uncertainty and demoralization—the Protestant work ethic values admired by Kaus will have at least a fighting chance.

Ah, but you say, think of the "unintended consequences." If welfare paid enough to allow people to live at some level of dignity and comfort, wouldn't all low-wage workers drop their jobs and come flocking to the Department of Social Services? Who would be left to fry our burgers, sweep our offices, and change our bedpans? People might begin to believe that they are worth something more than the current, sub-poverty minimum wage of $3.35 an hour.

But that is exactly the "consequence" we should be aiming for. The real problem is not welfare but the fact that an increasing number of jobs do not pay enough to subsist on. If the public sector gave the poor and dislocated enough to live on (through unemployment compensation as well as AFDC), the private sector would no longer be able to get away with coolie wages. Wages would rise, and pretty soon the work ethic would begin to make sense as something other than a bludgeon with which to beat up on the down-and-out.

2. JOBS PLUS COMPASSION
Robert Kuttner

Mickey Kaus takes a fundamentally good idea—full employment backed up by public jobs—and manages to make it punitive and churlish. He is glib about intractable problems like the dilemma of mothers of very small children. AFDC mothers won't cooperate by signing up for three-dollar-an-hour jobs? No problem, take away their kids! Perhaps neo-liberal social critics will adopt them.

Kaus is too hard on "soft workfare," but far too soft on the practical problems of implementing a sub-minimum-wage jobs program for semi-literate mothers of small children. As Kaus notes, work requirements have been a nominal part of welfare policy since 1967. Why, then, has nobody yet devised a "hard workfare" program tough enough to satisfy Kaus? Surely it isn't because AFDC mothers are a popular constituency, or because of those nefarious anti-poverty lawyers. It is because it's extremely difficult to motivate, or supervise work projects for, society's most troubled people without either spending a lot of money for support or letting the devil take the hindmost.

Nobody has ever operated anything close to a WPA for welfare mothers. The only such programs that have succeeded, in Kaus's terms, in instilling a work ethic have had two ingredients that Kaus disdains: a large element of what he snidely dismisses as "social work"—job training and personal supports. These have resulted in a real improvement in economic condition.

Massachusetts's ET is one such program. Yes, ET inflates its numbers, but it undeniably helps welfare mothers get out of the self-perpetuating cycle of dependence and into jobs far better than the three-dollar-an-hour ones Kaus proposes.

As Reagan's attempt to get tough with disability claimants proved, there is no surgical way to remove the borderline cases without hurting the deserving ones. Leaving work dropouts to the tender mercies of "soup kitchens" might compel some idlers to work at sub-minimum-wage jobs, but it would also make the ghetto an even bleaker, more alienated place and the society a nastier one.

Kaus also glosses over the effect of three-dollar-an-hour jobs on the labor market. There may be some fat left in the public sector, but there are many exemplars of the work ethic with $10,000- to $20,000-a-year jobs in state and local government. What happens to them when armies of the sub-minimum-wage workers sweep in? The public-employee unions would support a public-jobs program that paid a decent wage and offered the eventual prospect of permanent employment.

Liberals need to rehabilitate the worthy idea of public-service employment—but not as a cheap and punitive cure for the multiple pathologies of the black underclass. With a bit more compassion, Kaus's blueprint could be turned into a decent program. Suppose the public jobs paid four dollars an hour; suppose in the case of heads of households the government made up half of the difference between that wage and six dollars an hour, as Brandeis University professor Robert Lerman suggests. Suppose these jobs offered high school equivalency courses as a fringe benefit, for extra pay. Suppose they served as feeders into real civil-service jobs, or ET-style private-sector jobs. In short, suppose they offered the promise of improved lives, rather than just society's getting its pound of flesh. Then, and only then, it might make sense to put some time limit on AFDC benefits.

It is not hard to design, in Kaus's term, "authoritarian" systems of coerced work. But no known model of this approach is terribly attractive, or terribly liberal. Neoliberalism on the cheap adds up not to a work-ethic state; but to a forced-labor state.

3. MAKING ALLOWANCES
Sylvia Ann Hewlett

Mickey Kaus correctly identifies the lack of child care as a major obstacle preventing low-income single mothers from obtaining jobs. But creating a special system of day care for the poor would quickly degenerate into a custodial operation attracting neither significant public funding nor community support. The dramatic changes in American family life over the last several decades have made it clear that we need a much broader system of supports for the bearing and rearing of children.

Thirty years ago men represented 70 per cent of the work force. Today they make up only 55 per cent, and nearly 70 per cent of mothers with school-age children work outside the home, as do half of all mothers with children under one year old. Yet 60 per cent of working women have no rights to maternity leave when they give birth to a child, and the federal government is spending

25 per cent less money on child care than it did in 1980. Because of this lack of support, most women pay a big penalty when they become mothers—losing, on average, 20 per cent of their earning power in the two years following childbirth. Since most modern families rely heavily on female earnings, these penalties exert a substantial toll, not only on single mothers in the ghetto, but also on millions of working couples struggling to put together a decent standard of living.

One of the best-kept secrets is that family income in the United States has declined every year since 1973. (In 1973 median family income stood at $28,167; by 1984 it had dropped to $26,433.) Families with young children have been hardest hit. Many wives no longer can afford to quit their jobs when they have children. They need to stay in the labor force to help pay the rent and buy the groceries.

What we need is a new system of family supports that includes job-protected parental leave (along the lines of the bill currently before Congress [another bill was pending in May 1990]), flexible work schedules, an expanded system of pre-schools for three-, four-, and five-year-olds, and a generous child allowance for families with a household income of under $30,000 a year.

This allowance, consisting of $100 per month per child under the age of six, paid directly to eligible families, would accomplish a range of social policy goals: (1) It would demonstrate that we, as a nation, value children. (2) It would bring the income of welfare mothers above the poverty line without discriminating against the working poor or against intact, two-parent families. Too often social policies have targeted broken families without helping those with children who are struggling to remain viable in a hostile social and economic climate. (3) It would support child-raising while preserving private choice. Working parents could use the allowance to help pay for child care, or enable a parent to stay at home and raise the children in a more traditional manner.

The child-care allowance would not be prohibitively expensive. It could be partially paid for by eliminating the child-care tax credit, an inefficient and unfair way of subsidizing families, since the benefit mostly goes to professional women. The tax credit costs the federal government $2 billion a year. Total costs for a child-allowance program would be in the region of $5 billion to $10 billion a year, a small price to pay to bolster the security and stability of families with young children. A child allowance may be an innovation in America, but most Western democracies have some version of such a system in place.

A program of family supports with a child allowance as its centerpiece is one of the few policy initiatives that could capture the imagination of the electorate in this age of budget-cutting and limited social conscience. However serious the needs of the women and children on welfare, no acts will be passed and no money will be spent until we also address the needs of middle America. Too many families are pinching and scraping, while dealing with the agonies of latch-key children and third-rate day care. They have little appetite for new social programs, but would surely support a set of policies that improved family life across the board.

4. The Culture Club
William Julius Wilson

Mickey Kaus's policy agenda for "The Work Ethic State" is one of the most imaginative, persuasive, and realistic proposals that have been advanced to attack inner-city joblessness and welfare dependency. It is rather strange, therefore, that this thoughtful analysis is based in highly questionable claims about the existence and influence of a ghetto "culture of poverty." Kaus boldly asserts that no one "can doubt that there is a culture of poverty out there that has taken on a life of its own," most frequently citing Nicholas Lemann's *Atlantic* article on "The Origins of the Underclass" and Leon Dash's series in the *Washington Post* on black teenage pregnancy. These journalistic accounts are vulnerable when subjected to critical intellectual scrutiny.

As Kaus correctly points out, "Lemann stresses a fairly direct connection between those blacks who worked in the sharecropping system in the South and those who formed the lower class of the ghettos after the great migration north." But the systematic research on urban poverty and recent migration consistently shows that Southern-born blacks who have migrated to the urban North have lower unemployment rates, higher labor-force participation rates, and lower welfare rates than Northern-born blacks. This research, which includes four major studies since 1975, is not even mentioned by Lemann.

It is true that the presence of stable working- and middle-class families in the ghetto provides mainstream role models that reinforce values pertaining to employment, education, and family structure. But a far more important effect is the institutional stability that these families provide in these neighborhoods because of their greater economic and educational resources, especially during periods of economic stagnation.

It is also important to recognize that children growing up in neighborhoods in which the working and middle classes have departed thereby occupy different niches with respect to jobs, opportunities for marriage, and exposure to conventional role models. Take opportunities for marriage. Kaus refers to the Dash article when stating that teenage girls in the inner city "are often ridiculed by other girls if they remain virgins too long into their teens." Kaus argues that "once AFDC benefits reach a certain threshold that allows poor single mothers to survive, the culture of the underclass can start growing as women have babies for all the various non-welfare reasons they have them." However, the actual black teenage birth rate in 1983—that is, the number of live births per 1,000 women—was 35 per cent less than in 1970, and 40 per cent less than in 1960. How does the "culture of poverty" argument of black teenage childbearing explain this?

The real problem, you see, is not the rate of teenage childbearing, but the proportion of teenage births that are out of wedlock, which has substantially increased. One competing (and to my mind, more persuasive) explanation associates the increase in the ratio of out-of-wedlock births and the rate of female-headed families with the declining labor-market status of young black males, that is to say, the shrinking pool of marriageable—employed—black men.

Cultural values do not ultimately determine behavior or success. Rather, cultural values emerge from specific circumstances and life chances and reflect one's position in the racial-class structure. Thus, if underclass blacks have low aspirations or do not plan for the future, it is not ultimately the result of different cultural norms, but the product of restricted opportunities, a bleak future, and feelings of resignation originating from unpleasant personal experiences. Despite the claims of journalists about the ascendancy of an autonomous "culture of poverty," this fundamental principle has yet to be challenged by systematic academic research.

5. OUTSIDE THE GHETTO
David T. Ellwood

Mickey Kaus's "humane" cure for the "culture of poverty" loses much of its logic and humanity when one realizes that the "underclass," however it is defined, is but a tiny minority of the poor. The 1980 Census shows that less than 12 per cent of the poor female-headed families with children live in severe poverty areas (census tracts with poverty rates over 40 per cent) of large and moderate-sized cities. If we confined our analysis to blacks, as Kaus suggests we could, we'd be looking at less than 10 per cent of poor single mothers. These isolated and concentrated poor may be the most visible and troubled members of our society, but they are not typical of the poor.

Kaus does acknowledge that the "underclass embraces only a minority of the poor." Yet he still asks us to punish all welfare recipients because of frustration over the situation of a few. The group that would be hardest hit as a result would be single women with children, since most single persons without children and most male-headed families don't qualify for much assistance.

Kaus insists that all single mothers ought to work all the time in order to provide financial support for the family. Almost half of the children born today will spend some time in a single-parent home. So this proposal will be felt not only in the ghettos of America but also in the heartland.

Is it fair or desirable to ask all single mothers to provide all the support of the family? It is true that most married mothers are now working, but they most commonly work part time or part year. Less than 30 per cent of married mothers work full year, full time (as compared to 37 per cent for female family heads). Given the patterns for married mothers, it seems more than a bit extreme to insist that all single mothers work all the time. Kaus's approach does not allow a mother to work only part time, and in any case part-time work at less than the minimum wage would hardly feed the children, much less house or clothe them.

Instead, we ought to provide some sort of income supplement either through a guaranteed child-support payment (paid by the father with a minimum guaranteed by the government) or some sort of children's allowance. That plus a part-time job might give mothers a serious chance to escape welfare. Besides these income supplements, single mothers ought to be assured of at least several years of transitional public assistance: public assistance coupled with training and services.

Those who still were not self-supporting after these supplements and after the transitional assistance program would rightly command more serious concern. Only for this much smaller group is it logical even to consider "hard workfare" or guaranteed jobs without welfare or some form of more intensive and comprehensive aid. And workfare need not be as harsh as Kaus insists. With the other income supplements, part-time work is all that need be expected.

I do not share Kaus's conceptions of America's ghettos. I think he confuses the symptoms of deprivation, concentration, isolation, abysmal education, and limited opportunity with the causes. These areas need urgent and immediate assistance. Guaranteed jobs would probably help. But whatever one finds in the ghettos, they are not representative. Those who make poverty policy seeing only the black faces in Harlem commit as grave a sin as those who ignore those faces in the first place.

6. Not Only Work Works
Lawrence Mead

Mickey Kaus is right to say that the poor have to work. But I would disagree that everyone has to work immediately and that government has to provide all the jobs.

Kaus says that "only work works." But it is probably too tough on the employable recipients, and too tough politically, to expect all of them to work immediately. Many have never worked steadily, and they need some kind of preparation. Work programs will not pass, or survive, unless they have an important training dimension.

Nor is it necessary to avoid training to put people to work. What seems to motivate recipients is required participation of *some* sort. To judge from existing work programs, you can put people into either job search or training, and they will go to work, provided participation is mandatory. To obligate them to do *something* is more important than what it is. We should aim to maximize the percentage of employable recipients who have to do something active every day: either work or preparation for work. In its own work proposals, the Reagan administration wisely shifted from demanding immediate work for everyone to seeking higher participation levels.

You do have to keep training from becoming an escape from work, as it has sometimes been in the past. Training has to be for limited periods, after which clients have to accept even unpleasant jobs. Or require a work history as a prerequisite for training, and require that clients return to work regularly between periods of training. This ensures that they come to terms with the labor market as it is, and that they have the elemental work discipline needed to profit from training.

Kaus also relies unduly on government to provide the jobs for the recipients. The evidence is that low-paid private jobs are already available in most areas, even in cities where unemployment rates are high. Of course, employment cannot strictly speaking be guaranteed unless government provides it, but you need only a small pool of public jobs to do that. We need to emphasize private-sector job search and placement, and use the government slots as a backup. This is what most of the new AFDC work programs have done.

The danger with public jobs, especially if you create as many as Kaus wants, is that they are not real. They turn out to be less demanding than private positions, partly because the government faces no bottom line. Kaus's jobs would be low paid, but to judge from experience, transition out of them into the private sector would not "take care of itself." Rather, we should put most recipients to work out in the marketplace in the first place.

Kaus seems to have mixed a social-policy proposal with the traditional liberal goal of using government to improve on the private economy. The point of his public jobs seems to be to guarantee work in a humane form. Government may well treat disadvantaged employees better than private employers, who might be abusive.

But whatever the truth of these concerns, addressing them in a welfare program does not help the poor. The cause of equality requires that the poor be held to the same standards as other people. It is invidious to worry more about their working conditions than those of others. We already have laws to protect workers, all workers. If we want to improve working conditions or raise the minimum wage, we should do it for everyone, not just the poor.

Rather than use the poor as a stalking horse for collectivism, we should address their work problem in its own right. The way to solve it is to expect them to work, or get ready to work, in the kind of ordinary jobs that most other Americans do every day.

7. INFTTC

Charles Murray

Cutting through the muddle-headedness we have been hearing about workfare, Mickey Kaus tells us that a successful program has to do three things: The jobs must be real and must be treated that way; otherwise, we will reproduce the worst of the CETA projects, with people being taught how to avoid work, not do it. The benefits must be less than for comparable work in the private sector; otherwise we will broaden dependency (as well as play havoc with the labor market). And the system must be universal; its effectiveness depends on people's assuming that they can't evade it.

Kaus's system will work if it is implemented exactly as he prescribes. The catch is that the federal government cannot implement his system. Imagine what will happen if it tries.

A large proportion of the people who are supposed to participate

will be unemployable by the standards of the private sector, meaning that they won't show up for work regularly, won't get much
done when they do show up, will quit at any excuse. There is no
known technique for changing the work habits of large numbers of
such persons, even when military discipline is available. (See what
happened when the Army tried: "Losing Battle" by David Evans,
The New Republic, June 30, 1986.) The logic of Kaus's program is
that such behavior will be changed over time: if there is no
alternative to work, people will eventually become "job-ready."
He's right. But in the meantime, thousands of people will have to
be fired.

How? Ask the people who run existing work programs; the
answers are not encouraging. An intricate body of labor and welfare
law and a cadre of ACLU and Legal Services lawyers guarantee that
Kaus cannot construct a program that enforces work standards.
The program administrators will be lucky if they can require even
that people show up at the work site to qualify for their pay. And
lacking work standards, the program will fall apart.

Even if the work standards could be maintained, Kaus's program
would be gutted by the reflexive response that has done in every
other attempt to make public assistance less attractive than employment at low wages: "It's Not Fair To The Children" (INFTTC).

What is to be done with women who get fired or who refuse to
participate in the first place? Kaus again has the right idea: that's
their choice—let them survive as they may. But are we to let
children go hungry because their parents won't work? Of course
not. Are we to take such children from their parents? Of course
not. So a shadow benefit program will develop for those who don't
participate. Eventually these benefits will be equivalent to the work
benefits. Otherwise, INFTTC.

INFTTC also means that program jobs cannot be paid an
invariant wage. The concept of "pay" must give way to the concept
of "allowance." After all, a woman with five children cannot be
expected to subsist on a less-than-minimum wage: INFTTC. Allowances will vary according to family size and for families with even a
few children will exceed the amounts to be earned in the private
sector.

The universality rule is also doomed. In the first month after the

Kaus program is inaugurated, the network news will be jammed with features about infants left untended while mothers go to work, and about men who collapse on the job because the supervisors didn't believe their stories about bad backs. People will be exempted—first a few (those with really small children and really bad backs), then more (those with fairly small children and fairly bad backs). Soon anyone with a few smarts who can't get out of the work requirement just won't be trying very hard.

Two issues should be kept separate. The federal government knows how to give things, and therefore the government can provide less-than-minimum-wage work for the person who has tried his damnedest but just cannot find a job. The problems I have described are comparatively minor for people who want to work but cannot find a job. These people, however, do not make up the underclass.

What Kaus wants to do is bring members of that underclass back into participation in American society. His diagnosis of what is required is acute and brave. But he is asking the government to behave like a concerned friend or relative or neighbor or church congregation, helping while at the same time holding people responsible for their behavior. Governments cannot do that. They try, and the harder they try the more totalitarian they become, but they never succeed.

THE AUTHOR REPLIES
Mickey Kaus

What do I mean by saying there is a largely black "culture of poverty"? I don't mean cultural values are not "ultimately" (Professor Wilson's fudge word) the product of "restricted opportunities." I don't mean poor blacks are "ultimately" to blame for their own problems. I am talking not about cause or culpability but about *solutions*. Whatever the cause, and whoever is to blame, the culture of the ghetto has taken on a life of its own so that today opening up job opportunities isn't enough.

Wilson points out the declining ranks of employed ("marriageable") black men. Why is this? Wilson's lack-of-jobs explanation rings increasingly hollow these days, a time of intense regional labor shortages. Ehrenreich and Piven's complaints about $3.35 "sub-poverty minimum wage" jobs are two years out of date. Unskilled hotel janitors in Washington, D.C., can now get seven to eight dollars an hour. Even McDonald's often pays five to six dollars an hour. Yet ghetto unemployment rates are hardly budging. Employers say the ghetto youths who do apply for jobs are often unemployable, that they show up for one or two days and then quit. That's what I mean by a "culture of poverty." While local black leaders complain that their constituents can't get to jobs in the D.C. suburbs, suburban employers have come to rely on commuters from West Virginia and Pennsylvania, and on immigrants.

The best evidence against the liberal argument that only a lack of jobs, and not culture, accounts for poverty may be what happens when you propose offering jobs. Then other liberals like Robert Kuttner pop up to say, in effect, "You don't really expect those people to work, do you?" After all, they are "semi-literate." They are "difficult to motivate" and supervise.

The "culture of poverty" is bigger than Ehrenreich and Piven let on. Yes, only 10 to 15 per cent of people who ever go on welfare stay there for eight years or more. But they constitute *over half* the people on welfare at any one time—not a "tiny minority." The study proving this was conducted by David Ellwood and Mary Jo Bane, which is why I'm surprised to find Ellwood himself resorting here to another misleading statistical half-truth. Sure, only 12 per cent of poor female-headed families may live within the Census's stringent definition of a ghetto (in New York state it's 32 per cent). But the census was a snapshot in time. As he knows, most of the poor mothers who were caught in that snapshot weren't going to stay poor long. If you could look at the single mothers who *stayed poor for a long time*, you would undoubtedly find that a far greater percentage of them lived in underclass neighborhoods.

But, say Ellwood, Ehrenreich, and Piven, why punish the nice middle- and working-class women who rely briefly on welfare after a traumatic divorce by expecting them to take jobs as if they were long-term welfare mothers? That's a very good point. What it suggests to me is not that we should keep on subsidizing underclass culture in order to help the struggling divorcees, but that these two separate groups of people must be addressed by two separate programs. What makes the divorcees so appealing? Well, they tried to play by the rules—they got married, they or their husbands worked, and now they need only temporary help. So why not allow poor mothers (or fathers with custody of kids) half a year of cash "divorce insurance" for every two years they've lived in a family in which one member worked full time—up to a one-year limit on aid? That would help fugitives from working, intact families without supporting a welfare culture of women who have babies without thinking seriously of either working or marrying someone who works.

And what about that latter group, the core of today's underclass, which all the commentators except Wilson admit exists? My argument was simple: if they are offered work rather than welfare, single-motherhood will seem less appealing. I don't deny there are more generous (or "compassionate") programs than low-wage government jobs, but I claim we must balance concern for today's welfare mothers with the need to *deter* tomorrow's potential welfare mothers.

A welfare system that lumps together all single mothers will find itself unable to perform this deterrent function—if it does, "It's Not Fair To The Divorcees." Ellwood's sophisticated proposal founders on this rock. It's nice to offer an income supplement, plus training and "services," plus "several years of transitional public assistance," to mothers who might need welfare as a temporary crutch. But if you wait until those years of transitional assistance are over before considering anything as mild as "part-time" work-fare, you've already given a generous enough subsidy to the single-mother culture to sustain it. Ellwood has argued that even Murray's ruthless let-them-starve "experiment" would not discourage single-motherhood. If so, surely his own mild plan would not have a big impact.

Ellwood at least recognizes that eventually you have to get tough with one segment of the welfare population. Ehrenreich and Piven don't, so convinced are they of the morally uplifting properties of cash. Theirs is an exceptionally clear articulation of the check-mailing version of liberalism, a sort of Grad Student State in which everyone lives on money from Washington without any annoying work responsibilities.

If giving every person in the country $13,500, or $27,000, would cure the "multiple pathologies" of the underclass, then we should do it immediately. But if there *is* a poverty culture in which women expect that they will get pregnant without marrying, it is insane to offer them large sums of money, no strings attached, for doing just that. Free money has enough potentially corrosive effects on the work ethic of communities that already have one. I agree more with the Frances Fox Piven of 1971, who (with Richard Cloward) argued that AFDC was a nefarious ruling-class plot because "the relief check becomes a surrogate for the male bread-winner. The resulting family breakdown and loss of control over the young is usually signified by the spread of certain forms of disorder—for example, school failure, crime, and addiction."

Giving cash in the form of child allowances doesn't alter this equation much. The virtue of a child allowance (like that of the guaranteed income) is that it is available to two-parent, working families. The hope of both proposals is that nobody would stay single on welfare if she could get married and stay on welfare. But the culture of single-motherhood is now so far advanced that this is surely wishful thinking. The allowance Hewlett proposes—$100 a month per child—doesn't come close to matching current welfare levels and wouldn't bring mothers with no other income anywhere near the poverty line. If Hewlett supplements it (as I assume she would) with a conventional welfare program, then the combined package will still sustain the culture of single-motherhood. If she doesn't, she has in effect recommended a drastic cut in AFDC (from $8,400 a year, for a mother with two kids in California, to $2,400)—a Murrayesque proposal far less "compassionate" than mine.

The alternative to doling out cash is mandating work, or training for work. Mead says only a small pool of public jobs would be necessary to enforce a universal work requirement. If so, fine. He accuses me of lowering "standards" for the poor, but it is he who offers special treatment, in the form of training "options" that relieve the work obligation for those on welfare (while he offers no jobs or training to those not on welfare). His sensible restrictions might well prevent training from becoming a loophole. But I still fear that any "workfare" plan—offering a welfare "entitlement" and then trying to take it away if people don't work or train—will run into tremendous political and legal resistance at the "take away" stage. Better to offer only work in the first place.

Kuttner adds a variety of sweeteners to this basic idea. I too like Lerman's wage-subsidy idea; Kuttner must have dozed off during the part of my piece where I endorsed it. It is one reason why Ehrenreich and Piven are wrong when they charge my plan would do nothing serious about poverty. Lerman's subsidy would raise the effective wage of even my three-dollar-an-hour neo-WPA jobs to $4.50, or $9,360 a year—above the poverty line for a family of three. It would be a major boost for Ehrenreich and Piven's hard-working Burger King moms, in direct proportion to how hard they work. I wouldn't mind raising the subsidy even to Ehrenreich and Piven's $13,500 level, as long as it went only to those who work.

Kuttner also recommends raising the WPA wage to four dollars an hour. Since Lerman's subsidy would add one dollar to that, the net difference between Kuttner's compassionate, hope-inspiring plan and my punitive "forced labor state" turns out to be 50 cents an hour (five dollars vs. $4.50). OK, Kuttner, it's a deal. Now watch the unions fight our four-dollar compromise tooth and nail, as they did California's higher-paying workfare jobs.

The great weak spot of any WPA-type proposal is its potential for makework. Charles Murray (along with Mead) knowingly runs through most of the potential pitfalls. Yes, in order to make a jobs program work you'd have to prune the civil-service legalisms that prevent firing government workers. You'd have to resist creating a "shadow" dole. You'd have to spend the money for adequate day care (integrated with middle-class day care, as Hewlett suggests). You'd have to set up a fair system of determining who is and isn't disabled and endure the occasional press horror stories about the inevitable misclassifications. (The identical problem already occurs with the existing federal disability programs, which Murray has said he'd keep.)

But if a jobs program provided services and built things taxpayers could see (as the original WPA did), they would begin to *demand* that it be run efficiently, a powerful counterforce to the entropic tendencies Murray describes. His argument is the equivalent of saying we should never fight a war because the Pentagon might screw it up. Given that his alternative is a far nastier (and even less feasible) campaign of human attrition, this still seems to me one war worth fighting.

5

The Work Obligation

Lawrence M. Mead

Non-work is the immediate cause of much poverty and dependency today. There is still a tendency to see the poor simply as victims entitled to government redress. That view is plausible for elderly and disabled poor, whom society does not expect to work. But it is implausible for families headed by able-bodied people of working age, whom society does expect to work.

Much poverty is transient, and half of all welfare cases leave the rolls in under two years. I am speaking here mainly about the long-term cases, and especially the welfare mothers and absent fathers whose reluctance to work helps create entrenched dependency.

Most families go on welfare because of the breakup or non-marriage of parents, but non-work often keeps them there. Very few adults work while they are on welfare: only about 6 per cent of AFDC (Aid to Families with Dependent Children, the main federal welfare program) families had earnings in May 1982, though a higher proportion do sometime during a year. Work is least common for the long-term dependent: after two years on the rolls, fewer than 5 per cent of the mothers leave because of work or reasons other than remarriage.[1]

For most women who head families, work is quite simply the difference between going on welfare and avoiding it. Two-thirds of

Lawrence M. Mead is associate professor of politics at New York University. This article is abridged by permission from the Winter 1988 issue of *Policy Review*, a publication of the Heritage Foundation. The notes for this chapter begin on page 71.

the female family heads who do not work are on welfare, while only 7 per cent of those who work full-time are. A fifth to two-fifths of welfare mothers also leave the rolls through work, a route second in importance only to marriage.

Those who doubt the efficacy of work in combating poverty point to the working, not the non-working, poor. It is true that most poor families have some earnings, yet remain needy. But few of these families have members working fulltime.

For the vast majority of workers, poverty is uncommon or transient. To work substantial hours and still be poor, one must usually combine low wages with a large non-working family. True, almost a third of all jobs do not pay enough to keep a four-person family out of poverty, if only one parent works, but in most families both parents work. In fact, since so many families have more than one worker, fewer than a fifth of workers who work at or below the minimum wage actually live in poor families.[2] In general, low wages cause economic *inequality*, not poverty. Low working hours are a much more common cause of poverty and dependency.

A generation ago, many more of the poor were working. In 1959, 32 per cent of the heads of poor families were working full-time, and only 31 per cent did not work at all.[3] Many more workers simply could not get above the poverty line then because of low wages or racial discrimination. Moreover, many more of them were elderly and disabled. It was easier to argue that the poor were "deserving," the victims of adverse conditions over which they had no control.

Since then, formalized racial discrimination has ended, and economic growth has carried most adults and their families above the poverty line—provided they are working. The main problem for the remaining poor adults is that they do not work steadily. That has shifted the debate about the reasons for poverty. The policy debate about how to overcome poverty has also shifted from benefit levels to employment strategies. Policymakers recognize that to reduce non-work would reduce dependency among the people of working age. But should programs to that end focus on "barriers" to employment—lack of jobs, child care, and training—or on work obligations?

Too Few Jobs?

The high unemployment from the early seventies to the mid-eighties made it seem that the main cause of non-work was a shortage of jobs. The overall jobless rate touched 10 per cent in 1982–83, and much higher rates are routinely recorded for the groups most likely to be poor and dependent—minorities, women, and youth. Many take this as *prima facie* evidence that not enough jobs are available.

The economy of the 1970s and early 1980s was prone to recession, yet it also had to absorb an enormous glut of new workers. The huge baby-boom generation came of age, and more women sought employment than ever before. As a result, between 1970 and 1985 the labor force—those working or seeking work—grew by an astounding 38 per cent. Apparently, a tepid economy could not keep pace. Job-seekers outnumbered jobs, and in the scramble for employment, the poor and dependent inevitably lost out.

But this account is outdated. Unemployment has fallen to below 6 per cent. Whatever its troubles, the economy has created jobs on a scale never before seen. From 1970 to 1985, total employment grew by 28 million jobs, or 35 per cent, almost enough to match the growth in the labor force. Since the end of the 1981–82 recession, job growth has considerably outpaced the entry of new workers, which is slowing down with the "baby bust" that followed the baby boom.

Some critics say the new employment is no more than a symptom of the "deindustrialization" of America. Many of the new jobs pay less than traditional manufacturing jobs, and many are part-time. They tend to fall within the service sector, which includes work in restaurants and hotels, maintenance of buildings and equipment, and other support services for business. It is easy to dismiss such jobs as marginal. But the income that unionized steel and auto workers used to have is not a realistic income standard now that our economy faces stiff foreign competition.

Moreover, a decline in job quality cannot explain non-work. For, in the face of lower wages, one might expect people to work more rather than less in order to maintain their incomes. That is what most Americans have done. During the 1970s growth in real wages stagnated. Many women responded by seeking work outside the home for the first time. Many men took extra jobs. Average working hours rose. Only among poor and dependent people was there, in general, a flat or negative response. Work levels of welfare recipients rose hardly at all, even though benefits fell in real terms because of inflation. Poor blacks did not share in the great economic strides made by the black middle class during this period. Black men as a group reduced their labor-force participation rate from 77 per cent in 1970 to 71 per cent in 1985.

Some might say that recipients fail to accept low-paid employment because they have the alternative of welfare. In other words, jobs must pay more than welfare does before it is worthwhile to take them. But this argument assumes that recipients have to leave welfare if they work. Actually, of mothers entering the work force in the typical AFDC work program, about half still receive some assistance. Because of this supplementation, welfare mothers should actually be freer to take low-paid jobs than many other people. Welfare and work are mutually exclusive only for unemployed fathers (whom states may choose to cover under AFDC), who may not work more than 100 hours a month without losing AFDC eligibility. But they represent only a small part of the employable caseload.

Low-Skilled Labor Shortage

Across most of the low-skilled labor market, there is now a manifest labor shortage. Low-skilled jobs have become particularly hard to fill in suburban areas, where some employers have taken to transporting workers from inner-city areas at their own expense. Many are being forced to pay well above the minimum wage even for unskilled work. The presence of some six million illegal immigrants in the country, mostly in urban areas, is testimony that at least menial jobs must exist in many cities. Many restaurant and laundry owners say they simply could not operate without the illegals, because most citizens will not accept "dirty work."

To argue that not enough job opportunities are available today, one must contend that the poor are somehow walled off from the opportunities that clearly do exist. One such argument maintains that the labor market is "dual" or "segmented." Access to the preferred jobs is allegedly controlled by government, large firms, and non-profit institutions, which hire on the basis of externals such as race or educational credentials, not actual ability, and thus choose mainly the better-off. The poor are relegated to menial or service-sector jobs that are transient and poorly paid. Actually, research has not demonstrated that labor markets treat the low-skilled unfairly. A University of Michigan panel study of income dynamics showed that blacks and the low-skilled, as well as whites and the better-off, experience considerable economic mobility over time, both up and down the economic ladder.

Another theory is that there is a "mismatch" between most available jobs and the location or skills of the poor. As John Kasarda has shown, much employment has migrated to the U.S. Sunbelt or even overseas from the Eastern and Midwestern cities where most poor and dependent people live. Employment opportunities have also moved from inner cities to the suburbs, where urban job-seekers have difficulty reaching jobs because of inadequate public transportation and costly housing. These shifts have been most pronounced among manufacturing employers whose jobs—manual but well paid—offered the best opportunity to low-skilled workers. Of course, a "high-tech" economy based on finance, information, and computing has grown up in many central cities. But high-tech work, so the argument goes, demands employees with strong communication or technical skills, which most poor adults with their limited education do not have.

William Julius Wilson claims that such shifts go far to explain the extraordinary dysfunctions found in the inner city. In *The Truly Disadvantaged* (University of Chicago Press, 1987), he argues that old-fashioned racial discrimination has receded, but he attributes much of the urban social breakdown to a changing economy that has denied previously available opportunity to poor black men.

Unrealistic Job Expectations

One trouble with the mismatch theory is that employment today does not usually require advanced skills. Not everybody in the high-tech economy is a financier or a computer programmer. Though fields like these are the fastest growing, most hiring in the future, as in the past, will be for low- and medium-skilled workers, such as secretaries, janitors, retail clerks, and truck drivers. New York City is a center of the "information economy," but in 1981, 57 per cent of its employment required only a high school diploma or less. That was a decline of only 1 per cent since 1972.[4]

The notion of a spatial mismatch in the labor market has been undercut by studies of Chicago by David Ellwood, and of Los Angeles by Jonathan Leonard, showing that the need of inner-city blacks to commute to jobs in the suburbs is only a minor reason for their unusually high unemployment. Even when poor blacks live as close to jobs as white or Hispanic workers, many fewer of them work. It is also doubtful that the black poor are as concentrated or as isolated from the rest of society as Wilson suggests. According to recent research by Mary Jo Bane and Paul Jargowsky, these problems seem acute only in a few large cities, especially New York and Chicago.

Although cases of long-term joblessness attract the most attention, most of the unemployed remain out of work only briefly. More have quit their jobs or just entered or reentered the labor force than have been "thrown out" of work. This pattern of turnover, rather than steady work, is most pronounced for minorities, women, and youth, the groups with the highest unemployment. White, male, and older workers tend to hold the same jobs longer.

Surveys have shown that many unemployed lack jobs, not because they cannot find any, but because of the expectations they have about wages and working conditions. According to a Labor Department survey done in 1976, the average jobless person wants a 7 per cent raise to go back to work, and his demands drop below his previous wage only after almost a year out of work. Most unemployed are also unwilling to commute more than twenty miles to reach new jobs.[5] A person may remain unemployed by the official definition even if his expectations from the job market are totally unrealistic. The presence of unemployment, then, cannot be taken as proof that jobs are lacking.

Surveys focused specifically on the poor and dependent find

much the same. Among poor adults, only 40 per cent of those working less than full-time give inability to find work as the main reason, and only 11 per cent of those not working at all do so. For poor blacks the comparable figures are 45 and 16 per cent.[6] Other constraints, including health problems and housekeeping responsibilities, are more important, especially for non-workers. Inner-city black youth regularly record unemployment rates over 40 per cent, yet 71 per cent say they can find a minimum-wage job fairly easily.[7]

Welfare Mothers: Now Employable

Liberal reformers also say that welfare mothers face special difficulties in working. After all, AFDC was first instituted in 1935 on the supposition that mothers heading families were unemployable. They were supposed to stay home and raise their children. If we now demand that they work, government must first guarantee them child care.

But the surge of women into jobs has changed social norms. Welfare mothers can no longer be seen as unemployable now that more than half of female family heads with children under eighteen are working, nearly three-quarters of them full-time. For divorced and separated mothers like those on AFDC, the working proportion is nearly two-thirds. Welfare mothers are distinctly out of step. Only about 15 per cent of them worked in the thirteen years prior to the 1981 cuts in AFDC eligibility, which removed most working mothers from the rolls. This was so even though the mothers became more employable during that period—younger, better educated, and with fewer children (over 70 per cent have only one or two).

While children certainly make it difficult for mothers to work, they are not the hard-and-fast barrier that is often supposed. In fact, as high a proportion of single mothers work as do single women without children.[8] Even young children are not prohibitive. Welfare mothers with pre-school children are no less likely to work their way off the rolls than those with older children, and two-thirds of mothers who leave welfare this way still have children at home.[9]

The Need for Child Care

Working mothers certainly need child care, but they seldom rely on organized facilities such as government child-care centers. Only 9 per cent of primary child-care arrangements by working parents involved day-care centers or nursery schools in 1984–85. Even for the most dependent group, single mothers with children under five, the figure was only 27 per cent. Overwhelmingly, the parents rely on less formal arrangements, chiefly care by friends or relatives.[10] Apparently they arrange care fairly easily, as fewer than 6 per cent of the working mothers in a given month lose time on the job because of problems with their child-care arrangements.[11] In only 10 per cent of the cases is the availability of care critical to a mother seeking work; finding the right job is much more important.[12]

Child-care advocates claim that the parents would use more center care if it were available. But most mothers prefer informal arrangements, probably because they have more control over them. When government has offered free care in centers as part of social experiments, it has sometimes gone unused. Informal care is also much less costly than center care, which must satisfy elaborate government staffing and licensing rules.

There appears, in fact, to be little unmet need for child care. That is why proposals for a national day-care program covering the general population have always failed. Of course, government must *pay* for child care for welfare mothers if it wants them to work. It already does this, usually by adjusting the mother's grant, while they are on welfare. More funding for transitional care after they leave welfare may be needed. But government need not provide the care in its own facilities.

Training to Build Motivation

Finally, liberal reformers say that adult recipients can be expected to work only if they first receive training to raise their skills and earnings. Otherwise they either will fail to get jobs or, if they do get them, will not earn enough to get off welfare or out of poverty.

The benefits of training have been deduced from evaluations of some of the post-1981 work programs by the Manpower Demonstration Research Corporation (MDRC). These suggest that well-run training and jobs programs for recipients have the potential to raise their income by as much as 25 per cent, as well as reduce dependency.

But training is easily oversold. The earnings gains in even the best training programs are limited, seldom enough to get welfare families entirely out of poverty or off welfare. Furthermore, "training" can be a misnomer, as few programs raise the skills of adults on welfare, most of whom have shown little ability to learn in school. The main impact of training programs is not on job quality but on motivation—on causing the clients to work *more hours* in the rudimentary jobs they are already able to get.

The best training programs tend to be highly authoritative, aimed at impressing on clients a responsibility to work at whatever job they can get. Non-directive programs can actually depress work effort, as clients embark on unrealistic training programs for "better" jobs at the expense of immediate employment. Welfare employment programs have made that mistake in the past. They overinvested in training, only to see very few trainees go to work in available jobs.

Nor is training usually necessary for work. Welfare mothers average 2.6 years of work experience since they left school.[13] Many work "off the books" while they are on welfare, a dodge that work requirements help detect. Their problem is seldom that they are unemployable but rather that they do not work consistently.

Serious effort is required to find a job and to arrange one's private life for work. But these burdens do not seem notably greater for the poor and dependent than they are for low-skilled working people. What liberal reformers call "barriers" are mostly the ordinary demands of employment—demands that most working Americans cope with every day. Government could perhaps overwhelm these so-called barriers with benefits, guaranteeing jobs, child care, and training especially for the poor and dependent. But to do that would be unfair to many Americans who already work in menial jobs without special assistance. It would also be ineffective in integrating the poor, because they would not earn the respect of others. Work where government bears all the burdens without holding the employee accountable for performance is simply another form of welfare.

Non-Work: The Disincentives Theory

To explain non-work, it is more promising to look inside the poor than outside—to the mentality of those who have difficulty working. There have been three main psychological theories of non-work.

The most common, but least plausible, is that welfare recipients are deterred from working by the "disincentives" inherent in welfare. If they work, their earnings are normally deducted from their welfare grants. So why work? Some conservatives conclude that the poor will work only if welfare for the able-bodied is abolished. Liberals say the problems can be overcome with work incentives— a policy of deducting only part of a person's earnings from the welfare grant, thereby restoring at least some payoff to work. On this logic, Congress in 1967 decided to require AFDC recipients to deduct only about two-thirds of any earnings.

However, research has failed to discover more than a weak connection between welfare benefits levels and work effort by recipients. Work levels on welfare did not rise after work incentives were instituted, or when real benefits fell during the 1970s. The main effect of the incentives has been to expand eligibility for welfare and hence to increase costs, by allowing more working people to get on the rolls despite their earnings. For these reasons, in 1981 Congress withdrew most of the AFDC work incentive it had granted in 1967. Ellwood and Bane find that welfare disincentives have more impact on the structure of welfare families, by promoting divorce and especially by causing young unwed mothers to leave home and set up their own households.

One might still argue that the mere presence of welfare depresses work levels below what they would otherwise be. But in a world where welfare exists, variations in benefits and incentives have little further effect.

The disincentives theory is also implausible because of its economic logic. It assumes that the non-working poor are rational in the economist's sense, that they calculate what will serve their financial advantage and then act accordingly. But the mentality of most long-term poor people today is decidedly non-economic. Behaviors such as illegitimacy or crime may satisfy impulses, but they are not rational in any longer-run sense. Similarly, there is no way that non-work can rationally be regarded as self-serving—especially given the very real opportunities that exist in this country, even for the poor. If the poor were as sensitive to economic payoffs as the disincentives theory supposes, most would not be poor in the first place.

Non-Work: The Political Theory

A more persuasive theory is that non-work is political. Perhaps non-workers are not acting to maximize their incomes. They are protesting, by refusing to work, against the unattractive jobs the economy offers them. They demand that government force employers to pay them more or provide "better" jobs in government itself. To make that point, they will decline to work even though this is personally costly to them. Non-work, in this view, is analogous to a strike for better wages and working conditions.

This interpretation fits the behavior of many non-working men, especially ghetto youth. Members of this group do tend to see demands that they accept menial jobs as a denial of rights, a form of racial subjugation. They often resist direction by the staff of training programs, one reason they usually benefit less from training than do women. Black youth often refuse jobs that pay them less than white youth, even if this means they remain unemployed. Some welfare mothers say they should not have to take menial jobs, as domestics for example; they demand jobs with better pay and career prospects. Such feelings were aggressively voiced by the welfare-rights movement of the 1960s.

The problem with this view is that political action is supposed to be collective, open, and proud. Non-work seldom has these characteristics. Rather, it is individual and secretive, and the non-worker is frequently ashamed. Studies of the poor do not suggest that they are rebellious. Most, in fact, are deferential to all mainstream mores—to the despair of those who wish to see them as a revolutionary class. Most clients in workfare programs respond positively to the experience of being required to work. The majority accept the requirement as fair, and they feel they are contributing to society. They do not share the view, propagated by advocate groups, that workfare is negative and punitive, intended only to drive needy people off the rolls.

Non-Work: The "Culture of Poverty"

The difficulty with these economic and political theories of non-work is their assumption that behavior corresponds to considered intentions. If the poor do not work, either they are kept from doing so or they must not want to. The third and most plausible theory, especially for welfare mothers, may be called the "culture of poverty" theory, which says that aspirations can be radically inconsistent with behaviors. The poor *want* to work and achieve other orthodox values but feel *unable* to do so because of forces beyond their control. They would like to observe strictures such as obedience to law but feel they cannot in the circumstances they face. Social norms are held as *aspirations*, not as *obligations* binding on actual behavior.

The tragedy of low-income life is that a pathological culture in which the poor participate often overrides their good intentions. Parents want their children to avoid trouble but lose control of them to a street life of hustling and crime. Children want to succeed but lack the discipline to get through school. Girls want to marry and escape poverty but get pregnant and go on welfare. Youths want to "make it" but feel they can earn the money they deserve only by selling drugs.

Specifically, *the poor are as eager to work as the better-off, but the strength of this desire appears to be unrelated to their work behavior.* Whether they actually work depends, rather, on whether they believe they *can* and *must* work. If they have successfully held jobs in the past and/or accept low-level positions to begin with, they will probably know they *can* work. If they have not become dependent on welfare or illegal sources of income, they probably will accept the fact that to survive they *must* work. But simply the desire for employment is insufficient to make a person work. For those who do not accept these attitudes, work remains an aspiration, neither achievable nor required.

Disadvantaged clients in work programs often will accept work only if government first assumes most of the burdens of achieving it. They want the programs to arrange child care and transportation, provide training, and, above all, guarantee attractive jobs in advance. But government cannot afford these burdens. And even if it could, guaranteed "employment" would not really be work, because it would not impose any real responsibility on the client. Work that is only a benefit, not an obligation, is welfare in disguise. The welfare mentality that expects everything from government is a greater barrier to employment than any practical impediment the needy face.

The federal government learned this lesson during the 1970s, when it tried to provide government jobs for the poor on a large scale. As many as 750,000 positions a year were funded under the Comprehensive Employment and Training Act (CETA). This "public service employment" (PSE) was supposed to allow disadvantaged workers to experience "success" in relatively comfortable, well-paid jobs arranged by government in local agencies. It was hoped that they would grow more accustomed to work and then make the transition to regular employment.

But few did. After their CETA jobs ended, most clients went on unemployment or welfare, entered another training program, or left the labor force instead of taking a regular job. In 1977, only 22 per cent of disadvantaged PSE clients "graduated" from the program, less than half of them for unsubsidized jobs, and most of those, like the PSE positions themselves, were in the public sector.[14] The hitch was that the private jobs these workers could command offered them nothing like the pay and security they had known in government. Real work will always be tougher than a guaranteed job. That disappointment as well as other controversies—particularly the diversion of slots to support regular municipal employees—persuaded Congress to kill PSE in 1981.

The Core Conviction: Not Responsible

At the core of the culture of poverty is the conviction that one is not responsible for one's fate, what psychologists call inefficacy. The long-term poor tend to feel that success or failure depends, not on their own efforts or lack thereof, but on arbitrary forces beyond their control. If they fail in school or on the job, they are more likely than the better-off to attribute it to the undeserved hostility of teachers or supervisors, or to racial discrimination, even if personal behavior is really to blame.

Inefficacy seems to be the result primarily of weak socialization. Because of erratic parenting, many poor children fail to internalize goals such as work and self-reliance with enough force to feel them as obligations. The parents themselves have often been unable to control their own lives. Welfare mothers who are dependent a long time often grew up in female-headed families; and youth who do not work often come from families living on welfare or in public housing.[15]

These psychological theories illuminate the real character of the work problem. Few poor adults, outside the disabled, are literally unemployable, but a great many have problems of work discipline. They find work with little more trouble than other people, but they have a great deal more trouble keeping it. They quit low-paid jobs rather than sticking with them long enough to earn raises and qualify for better positions. The problem is partly rejection of the available jobs, but mostly an inability to *commit* themselves to them. The long-term poor never get their feet solidly on the bottom of the economic ladder and therefore can never climb it.

The Enforcement Theory

Employment programs aimed specifically at the poor and the disadvantaged have shown little impact, mainly because they asked, and got, little commitment from their clients. The error of federal incentives, training, and jobs programs was that they offered only benefits in one form or another, without firm work requirements. All assumed that opportunity was the main problem. All attempted, in one way or another, to raise wages per working hour, as if low wages were the major cause of poverty. None directly confronted the greater problem—the low number of hours that the poor work.

Policymakers have begun to acknowledge that work must be enforced as are other civilities, such as obedience to the law or payment of taxes. Work serves important social values, and dependent adults should be required to work. Whereas the barriers theory says the poor are blocked from work and need greater freedom, the enforcement theory says they are in some ways too free. The solution to the work problem lies in obligation, not in freedom. Social policy has slowly moved in the direction of work enforcement. In 1967, employable welfare recipients were required to register with employment programs for possible work or training, and since then the requirements have become steadily more stringent. Recent welfare employment programs have recorded favorable evaluations, and they have shown more power to raise actual work effort by the poor than any other policy. As a result, the most recent reform of welfare, in 1988, took steps to expand these programs further.

Requirements suit the irresolute mentality of the poor: they want to work but feel they cannot. Enforcement operates to close the gap between the work norm and actual behavior, and changes work from an aspiration to an obligation. It places the employable poor in a structure, combining supports and requirements, where they find that they *must* do what they want to do, which is to work.

NOTES

1. June A. O'Neill et al., "An Analysis of Time on Welfare," study prepared for the U.S. Department of Health and Human Services (Washington, D.C.: Urban Institute, June 1984), pp. 27–28.

2. Robert D. Reischauer, "Welfare Reform and the Working Poor," unpublished paper, pp. 5–6, 22.

3. U.S. Department of Commerce, Bureau of the Census, *Characteristics of the Population Below the Poverty Level: 1984*, Series P-60, No. 152 (Washington, D.C.: U.S. Government Printing Office, 1986), table 4, p. 15.

4. Thomas Bailey and Roger Waldinger, "A Skills Mismatch in New York's Labor Market?," *New York Affairs*, vol. 8, no. 3 (Fall 1984), pp. 3–18. The study Bailey and Waldinger cite classifies jobs requiring a high school diploma or less as low-skilled unless they require at least eighteen months of pre-employment training.

5. Martin Feldstein and James Poterba, "Unemployment Insurance and Reservation Wages," *Journal of Public Economics*, vol. 23 (1984), pp. 147–50; Carl Rosenfeld, "Job Search of the Unemployed, May 1976," *Monthly Labor Review*, vol. 100, no. 11 (November 1977), pp. 39–43; Anne McDougal Young, "Job Search of Recipients of Unemployment Insurance," *Monthly Labor Review*, vol. 102, no. 2 (February 1979), pp. 49–54.

6. U.S. Department of Commerce, *Characteristics of the Population Below the Poverty Level: 1984*, table 10, pp. 37, 46.

7. Richard B. Freeman and Harry J. Holzer, "Young Blacks and Jobs—What We Now Know," *The Public Interest*, no. 78 (Winter 1985), p. 27.

72   LAWRENCE M. MEAD

8. Robert Moffit, "Work and the U.S. Welfare System: A Review," study prepared for the U.S. Department of Health and Human Services, February 1987, table 4.

9. Mary Jo Bane and David T. Ellwood, "The Dynamics of Dependence: The Routes to Self-Sufficiency," study prepared for the Department of Health and Human Services, June 1983, pp. 11–12, 33–35, 51; O'Neill et al., "Analysis of Time on Welfare," pp. 11–12, 43. Bane and Ellwood find the mother with preschool children more likely to work her way off, O'Neill et al. less likely to, than the mother with older children, probably because of different data.

10. U.S. Department of Commerce, Bureau of the Census, Who's Minding the Kids: Child Care Arrangements, Winter 1984–85, Series P-70, No. 9 (Washington, D.C.: U.S. Government Printing Office, May 1987), table 1.

11. Ibid., table 2.

12. Suzanne H. Woolsey, "Pied-Piper Politics and the Child Care Debate," Daedalus, vol. 106, no. 2 (Spring 1977), p. 138.

13. O'Neill et al., "Analysis of Time on Welfare," p. 29.

14. Congressional Budget Office, CETA Reauthorization Issues (Washington, D.C.: U.S. Government Printing Office, August 1978), pp. 17–19.

15. O'Neill et al., "Analysis of Time on Welfare," pp. 12–13, 35–36, 83–84; Freeman and Holzer, "Young Blacks and Jobs," p. 29.

6

How Social Policy Shapes Behavior

Charles Murray

A continuing problem clouds debate about the underclass. On one side are scholars like myself who include welfare among the causes of illegitimacy and chronic unemployment. Our accounts have generally been expository and speculative. On the other side are scholars who say that welfare *per se* does *not* cause illegitimacy and chronic unemployment. Their accounts have generally been quantitative and presented as refutations of the critics.

The defenders of welfare's good name are in a sense correct: welfare all by itself isn't really the problem. But neither has the debate been joined. The models they "test" are stick-figure caricatures.

If those of us who are critics of welfare do not like the way the defenders deal with our arguments, what approach would we propose instead?

Illegitimate births in poor communities are perhaps the most crucial of the problems associated with the underclass, and they provide a case in point that I will use here. My approach could also be used to explore the reasons behind chronic unemployment, delinquency, and drug dependency.

Charles Murray is a senior fellow at the Manhattan Institute for Policy Research. This article is reprinted by permission of the author from the Summer 1986 issue (number 84) of *The Public Interest* (© 1986 by National Affairs, Inc.). The notes for this chapter are on page 83.

THE "BRIBE" MODEL

The implied causal model that virtually all defenders of the welfare system use is one in which payment under the Aid to Families with Dependent Children program (AFDC) causes women to get pregnant and have babies. One direct cause, one direct effect. Women get pregnant to get money, and the larger the welfare reward, the more children single women will have. If the reward is reduced, the number of births will be reduced. Such hypotheses are easy to knock down, given such facts as (1) illegitimacy rates are similar in states that have widely varying AFDC payments and (2) the illegitimacy ratio continued to rise in the 1970s even though inflation was eroding the real value of AFDC benefits.

But that model is a caricature. Suppose that instead of asking, "Does welfare cause illegitimate births?," and then rushing to find a measure, we stand back and contemplate why on earth a single young woman with no income would conceive, carry a fetus to term, and then keep the baby to raise when she has other options available to her (abstention, contraception, abortion, marriage, adoption) at each step of the process.

Let me suggest an alternative model with three successively more complex, but also more realistic, variations.

THE "ENABLING" MODEL

There is no mystery about why a young woman might want to have a baby. Nature has made her physically ready for intercourse and pregnancy, and she may well believe that a baby will bring her love and fulfillment. For a poor young woman who has not been indoctrinated with the moral imperative of marriage, who is not going to college, and who is not going to have an interesting job, why not have a baby? Why not do this natural thing?

Viewed in this light, welfare does not *bribe* poor women to have babies, it *enables* them to do so. For the young woman who is not pregnant, "enabling" means that she does not ask, "Do I want a welfare check badly enough to get pregnant?," but rather, "If I happen to get pregnant, will the consequences really be so bad?" For the woman who finds herself pregnant, the question becomes more poignant: "Even though I do not have a husband and do not have money, am I really forced to abort this child or give it away?"

If "enabling" is a more realistic conception than "bribe," several testable implications seem to follow. One is that the concept of "enough" comes into play. At some very low level, the welfare package is so small that no woman will think she can support a baby on it. If every woman had precisely the same threshold definition of "enough," then illegitimacy ratios would be discontinuous as the welfare package increased. It is more reasonable to assume that women's threshold definitions are different but bunched within a relatively small range, so that at some point there is a bump in the "enabling effect" as the welfare package reaches a point where any poor woman can reasonably decide that the package is large enough for her to take care of the baby by herself if she must.

Another implication is that the focus on AFDC as a synonym for "welfare" is wrong. The appropriate measure of welfare will be not the size of the AFDC payment (the bribe) but the size of the welfare package (the enabler). What counts is not where the money comes from but whether the total resources are enough to get along. Still another implication is that a great deal will depend on whether a young woman *perceives* that the money is enough to enable the behavior. Thus, for example, calculations are likely to be based in part on local standards of living and whether other women in the neighborhood are managing to get along, not just on the raw purchasing power of the welfare package.

The Total Welfare Package

These implications, which seem straightforward and unremarkable, drastically change the way that one appraises the available data. If welfare *bribes* single women to have babies, then it makes sense to compare the illegitimacy rates in stingy AFDC states and generous AFDC states and to be surprised that there is little difference. But if welfare *enables* single women to have babies, the comparison focuses on the total welfare package. With so many sources of cash and in-kind welfare, the total package has become difficult to measure, but the General Accounting Office did it in 1978, with surprising results. Despite the dramatic differences in the size of AFDC payments across states, differences in the value of *the total package* were modest.

Using the GAO's example, poor young women in a stingy AFDC location (New Orleans) and in a generous AFDC location (San Francisco) were looking at nearly identical choices relative to the local economy. As of 1978, the portion of the local median household income provided by the welfare package was 66 per cent in New Orleans and 65 per cent in San Francisco.[1] Moreover, in both cases the raw amount of local purchasing power is plausibly beyond the threshold of "enough" for a reasonably poor woman— in 1978, according to GAO estimates, more than $10,000 a year for a San Francisco woman with a baby and almost $8,000 for a New Orleans woman.

It is no surprise, then, that one finds little difference between the illegitimacy ratios in California and Louisiana. Nor should it be surprising that erosion of the real value of AFDC payments has had little effect on illegitimate birth ratios. As long as poor women perceive the total welfare package as "enough," they might reasonably choose welfare as a means of doing something they might, *ceteris paribus*, like to do anyway. Inflation in the 1970s and 1980s has left the total benefit package well above a plausible threshold of "enough."

In contrast, during the 1960s there was a very large change in the size of the welfare package. In 1959, when the welfare package was essentially limited to AFDC, the average payment provided only 25 per cent of the median income in Louisiana and 29 per cent in California. Nationwide, the average annual total payment to AFDC families in 1959 was only $1,300—less than $3,000 even in 1978 dollars. Furthermore, in 1959 (unlike 1978) this amount could not be supplemented by income from a job, and the woman could not live with a man without risking the loss of all her benefits. It would be no surprise if a reasonable poor young woman in 1959 thought that, all in all, the welfare package failed to reach the threshold of "enough."

It may be noted for the record that time-series analyses that match illegitimacy against welfare benefits conclude that welfare is the villain after all.[2] But my point is not to defend any particular analysis. Rather, I am suggesting that the data being used to prove that welfare is innocent are not exculpatory once they are considered in light of a model that more closely reflects the way a real, live young woman who is pregnant and poor might look at the welfare option. But putting the issue in terms of a "real, live young woman" brings us back to the need to broaden the model beyond the direct effects of welfare payments on the utility functions of young women. A real, live young woman is going to be affected by all sorts of other things as well.

VARIANT 1: ADDING IN MEN

Chief among these other things is likely to be a man. At the same time that women were becoming enabled to support a chld without having to rely on a man, men in poor communities were becoming less reliable. A realistic model must consider the possibility that these two phenomena are related. George Gilder was one of the first to state what the relationship might be, arguing that in poor communities a major effect of welfare has been to change the male role and consequently to change male behavior.[3]

At an individual level, a man uses a woman's welfare as a way of getting along—sometimes wholly off the woman, probably more often using the woman's apartment and other benefits as a supplement to his own income. At the least, he is not compelled to support the child in the household. This makes it easier for him to leave a job, to behave in ways that get him fired, or to delay acquiring a new job, all of which contribute to his longer-term unemployability.

At a community level, the hypothesis is that the existence of a large number of women on welfare leads to changes in peer values among young men. Getting a woman to support you confers status. Conversely, the status formerly associated with "being a good provider" disappears. Even when the man is employed, he is not the pillar of support for the family; the welfare system is. Gilder further argues that these conditions have profound psychological implications for males.

To simplify a rich argument: The existence of an extensive welfare system permits the woman to put less pressure on the man to behave responsibly, which facilitates irresponsible behavior by the man, which exacerbates his sense of superfluity and his search for alternative definitions of manliness. When welfare recipients are concentrated, as they are in the inner city, these dynamics create problems that extend far beyond the recipients of welfare. Community values and expectations of male behavior are changed, and with them the behavior of young men and women who never touch an AFDC check. The defenders of the welfare system are prone to sanitize their estimates of effects: when a single young woman in the inner city has a child and does not go on welfare (as often happens), it is inferred that welfare is not implicated in the behavior. This set of hypotheses argues otherwise, focusing on the fact that she *does* bear the child.

VARIANT 2: ADDING IN SCHOOLS AND CRIME

But welfare all by itself is not the problem. In trying to develop a model that approaches reality, we must deal with a proposition that has barely been recognized, let alone tested, in the debate over the underclass. The environment in which a young poor person grew up changed in several mutually consistent and interacting ways during the 1960s. The changes in welfare and the changes in the educational environment reinforced each other. Together they changed both the incentive structure facing young people and the status rewards associated with behaviors that make escape from poverty possible. In this third version of the model, these additional hypotheses seem especially important.

Schools: Loss of Deterence

One obvious hypothesis regarding education is that the deterioration of inner-city education left girls with fewer perceived options to compete with having a baby. The less obvious hypothesis is that a series of reforms crippled an important deterrent function that schools formerly served and instead facilitated the fashionability of teenage pregnancy.

Schools in poor neighborhoods traditionally have been a *primary dispenser of status rewards* for youngsters, from the prestige of being a cheerleader to the prize of a high school diploma. Schools also formerly served as the *validator of conventional morality*. A female student who was pregnant or had a child was, at the least, stigmatized and was often expelled in disgrace. In treating her this way, the school deterred pregnancy by girls who wanted to get a diploma or who were fearful (as most adolescents are) of being separated from their friends. It buttressed a united front of institutional disapproval (along with parents and church) among the institutions likely to play the largest roles in an adolescent's socialization. And by expelling pregnant girls, the school physically segregated the girls who did not get pregnant from the day-to-day classroom and schoolyard influence of girls who did.

Beginning in the mid-1960s, a concentrated effort was made by the reformers to keep schools from acting in these punitive ways toward pregnant girls, and these efforts were largely successful. Indeed, many inner-city schools now provide special services available only to pregnant girls and young mothers. If, as is commonly reported, getting pregnant has become a high-status thing to do in some inner-city schools, the phenomenon may not be completely mysterious. Schools once helped make such behavior scandalous and exacted the kinds of prices that adolescents are loath to pay; now, they do not.

The Increase in Crime

In inner-city communities where the increase in crime was greatest, the hypothesized effects of this increase on illegitimacy are at once indirect and large. At a specific level, access to income from the underground economy influences the role of men. A man who can make money from a hustle is less attached to the labor force, is more likely to end up in jail, and is not the kind of man that a pregnant young woman of sense will rely on. She might, with good reason, decide it is better for her to rely on welfare than to pressure such a man into marriage.

At a more general level, a community that subsists on illegal sources of income and is victimized by widespread violent crime is socially disorganized in crucial ways. To put it roughly, the good folks no longer set the standards. In some cases they are physically intimidated from setting standards (witness the situation in many housing projects); in others, the role models for the youth are not blue-collar working men who raise families but hustlers. In such communities, the social stigma against illegitimacy that used to exist in poor working communities is impossible, because in lawless communities the people whose values would produce that stigma cannot be in control. The soaring crime rate in the late 1960s is not irrelevant to the soaring illegitimacy ratio.

These hypotheses already exceed the capacity of quantitative policy analysis. It is hard to imagine, for example, that anyone can trace with structural equations the web of connections that might link policy changes in law enforcement, increases in crime, losses of informal social control, changes in norms, and increases in illegitimacy ratios. My purpose here, however, is not to establish the questions that might be answered, but to suggest questions we ought to keep in mind as we examine smaller pieces of the puzzle. James Q. Wilson made a similar point when he argued that the development of character in the citizenry must be a central concern of public policy, despite the looming difficulties of its being so.[4]

VARIANT 3: ADDING IN CHARACTER FORMATION

In that spirit, let me suggest a fourth elaboration of the welfare model. The hypothesis is that the effect of the social reforms of the 1960s on a specific problem such as illegitimacy springs not only from discrete changes in incentives and status rewards but also from a larger effect on the formation of character among poor young people, and especially black poor young people.

Perhaps the best place to start is with the young people themselves. Three patterns of behavior are familiar to the teachers, pediatricians, probation officers, and social workers who work with poor youths. One is that of the passive bystander. Two pediatricians put it this way: "One of the most difficult and frustrating scenarios faced by the practitioner who works with adolescents is the fifteen- or sixteen-year old who comes to find out if she is pregnant. When asked what she will do if she is, she replies, 'I dunno.' When asked what she will do if she is not pregnant, one gets the same response—with perhaps a 'nothin' different' added."[5] A second pattern is that of the youngster who refuses to acknowledge that anything is her fault. Somebody or something else is always to blame, no matter what the nature of her transgression, including pregnancy. She is not just inventing these excuses; she really believes that to hold her responsible is an injustice.

The third and in many ways the most worrisome pattern involves the poor youngster who is not a "problem" in the usual sense. She may study hard in school and have high intelligence, but she has almost no working understanding of the relationship of cause and effect in daily life. Her aspirations are vaulting—she wants to go to Harvard, wants to be a surgeon—but she does not understand what it takes to get from here to there. She has very little sense of the standards that apply in the outside world; she does not understand that thoughts of Harvard are absurd if she has never read anything but comic books. She thinks in terms, not of a sequence of outcomes leading to a goal, but of one great big outcome that will or won't occur. Most characteristically, she exhibits very little belief that she is in control of her destiny—that *her* decisions about *her* behavior will affect *her* future. In her own way, she is as passive as the pregnant teen-ager who says "I dunno" and as convinced of her own inefficacy as the hostile excusemaker.

Character and Policy

This brings us back to the relationship of character to social policy. A central element of good character, as Wilson used the term, perhaps the fundamental element, is acceptance of personal responsibility in two related but distinct senses. The first is the belief that one controls one's own behavior and, in general, controls one's own destiny—"internal locus of control," as psychologists call it. The other is the obligation to bear the consequences of one's own actions.

The disparate reforms of the 1960s shared (in varying ways and degrees) an assumption that people are *not* in control of their own behavior and should *not* properly be held responsible for the consequences of their actions. The economic system is to blame; the social environment is to blame; perhaps accidents and conceivably genetics are to blame; but people—specifically the poor and disadvantaged—are not to blame. They are victims in the grip of larger forces. Rhetorically, this message was conveyed most loudly and emphatically to black youths.

The reforms translated this message into specific policies, each with its own effect. A shadow effect of public housing is that a child grows up in a world where the decision about where one lives is in the hands of an anonymous housing authority. A shadow effect of reforms to keep youthful offenders out of correctional institutions is to blur the link between wrong behavior and bad consequences. A shadow effect of reforms to deemphasize testing in schools is to take away a template for measuring the results of one's efforts. The list could go on and on. Take virtually any legislation, administrative change, or Supreme Court decision of the 1960s and early 1970s intended to help poor people and ask, "How would this affect a poor young person's perception of his personal responsibility?," and the answer would be the same. Right behavior, he would learn, is not necessarily followed by rewards; wrong behavior is not necessarily followed by penalties. Outcomes are a lottery. When things go wrong, there are ready excuses; when things go well, it is luck.

To pursue this line of inquiry, it is not necessary to toss out alternative explanations. The *Zeitgeist* of the 1960s and a variety of other forces having nothing to do with social policy were surely at work. But these other forces have ebbed for most classes in our society or have been displaced by countervailing trends, while the rules set up for poor people in those years still operate largely unchanged. In many respects, social policy toward the poor is the last redoubt of the elite wisdom of the 1960s.

The kinds of hypotheses raised here need not be abruptly tested and then either accepted or discarded. They will not statistically test the validity of anti-poverty programs. They are more useful for the perspectives they provide. These hypotheses deal with the complicated side of the welfare problem: human behavior. Ways to shrink the underclass, when such ways are found, will grow from a strategic understanding of how social policy shapes behavior. To get leverage, analysts of social policy badly need a place to stand.

NOTES

1. Based on a GAO study of 1978 benefit levels, "Public Assistance Benefits Vary Widely from State to State, But Generally Exceed the Poverty Line" (Washington: Government Printing Office, November 14, 1980), pp. 19–20.

2. See, for example, C. R. Winegarden, "AFDC Effects on Illegitimacy Ratios: A Granger-Causal Analysis," Working Paper UT-86–01, University of Toledo.

3. George Gilder, *Visible Man* (New York: Basic Books, 1978).

4. James Q. Wilson, "The Rediscovery of Character: Private Virtue and Public Policy," *The Public Interest,* no. 81 (Fall 1985), pp. 3–16.

5. Robert W. Blum and Michael D. Resnick, "Adolescent Decision Making: Contraception, Abortion, Motherhood," *Pediatric Annals,* no. 11 (October 1982), p. 797.

7

The "Welfare Mentality": Insider Views

Ken Auletta

"Man, you go two, three years not working and hanging around and smoking reefer or drinking and then you get a job—you can't handle it. You do two, three weeks of idleness and after the first two, three weeks of working, you feel people are pushing you. You say, 'I don't want to get up in the morning, get pushed and shoved. I'm gonna get on welfare.' Unless a man sits down and gives it good thought, he's not gonna figure out how he got there. He's gonna fall into the same cycle."— William Block, class member, Basic Typing-27.

INTRODUCTION *This chapter is abridged from Ken Auletta's 1982 book* The Underclass. *The book traces the experiences of twenty-two participants in a supported-work training program in New York City run by the Wildcat Service Corporation. Wildcat was part of a national demonstration of Supported Work managed by the Manpower Demonstration Research Corporation, a non-profit organization that designs and evaluates innovative employment, education, and training programs for disadvantaged young people and adults.*

The Wildcat program, says Auletta, offers "counseling, training, and a one-year job to ex-convicts, ex-addicts, long-term welfare recipients, school dropouts, and delinquent youths—the core of the underclass. . . . After working on a supervised job in the private or government sector for five months, the members of this class—called Basic Typing-27—came to the West 37th Street training center to learn not just English, math, and typing but how to use an alarm clock and telephone, follow dress codes, cash checks, say please and thank you, tell the truth about their pasts, write letters, conduct job interviews."

Auletta sat in on the "life skills" class for seven months in 1980. The excerpt to follow deals with just one session of this class. Before the excerpt begins, the students are identified in brief biographies condensed from Auletta's descriptions of them. He did not use their real names.

The instructor for the life skills class was **Howard Smith**, 39, an ex-convict and former heroin and cocaine addict, drug peddler, and welfare cheat. While in prison for selling heroin he earned a high-school-equivalency diploma. After being released to a halfway house, he was eventually able to overcome his addiction and was given a job as a drug-abuse counselor at a rehabilitation center.

William Block, 28. A high school dropout, he married and had a son at seventeen. After his son died and his marriage failed, he began to drink and killed someone in an argument. Released from prison after two years, he was unable to find work and went on welfare.

Denise Brown, 28. Attractive and well-dressed, she was the eldest of ten children and was "like a second mother, which I couldn't handle, because I was so young," she says. After her parents divorced, another man who she says was violent and a child molester lived in the house. She fled to New York. She worked for the Post Office but was charged with embezzlement and spent three years on probation. She now wants to become an air-traffic controller.

Pearl Dawson, 45. A well-dressed woman who conscientiously completes class assignments, she is determined to get off welfare. Although she did well in high school, she gave birth to a child and did not graduate. After a divorce and unsuccessful remarriage, she began to drink heavily. In a drunken rage she knifed a woman fatally. She served eighteen months for manslaughter and was referred to Wildcat by her parole officer.

Leon Harris, 29. The youngest of eleven children, he began earning a living as a "stick-up kid" while still a teenager. At 22 he went to prison for armed robbery. Released after five years, he got involved in drugs, alcohol, and gambling, and went back to jail for narcotics possession. After his second release, a parole officer introduced him to Wildcat.

John Hicks, 22. Hicks reads at a tenth-grade level (high for Wildcat participants), has a high-school-equivalency diploma, and is the only married class member. He served six months in prison for violating probation. He plans to take the civil-service test and go to college.

Willy Joe, 24. His mother moved her five children from the

South to New York after his father abandoned them. He was close to his mother, but she died of cancer. He dropped out of school, became addicted to drugs, straightened out, but turned to crime. After being sentenced to five years for armed robbery, he was released after ten months.

Ramon Lopez, 32. When his family moved to New York from Puerto Rico, he couldn't keep up with English in school and was demoted two grades. He says that school taught him "I was dumb." Eventually he quit. After a two-year stint in the Army, he began using drugs, bought a gun, and was sent to jail for three years. Then, unable to find steady work, he went on welfare. He has never had a job longer than seven months.

William Mason, 37. One of nineteen children, he himself now has nine children and eleven grandchildren. As a teenager, he says, he "wanted to cut loose" and "always wanted to be a fighter." He spent thirteen months in prison for narcotics possession and says he now "wants to be a success."

Gladys Miller, 28. Hooked on heroin while in high school, she dropped out. She received a $5,000 insurance settlement after a car accident, but instead of using the money to marry and relocate in the South, as she had planned, she spent it all on drugs within two and a half weeks. She has lived with three different women, all on welfare, and says she "got into being gay by messing with drugs."

Mohammed (Jerome Patterson), 23. His mother brought her three children to New York from Georgia; he doesn't know who his father was. The family became dependent on welfare. The first of his many arrests came when he was twelve, for purse-snatching. He was sent to three reform schools, a mental institution, and later to prison, first for attempted murder and then for armed robbery. During his second term he became a convert to the Nation of Islam. He wants to become an architectural draftsman.

John Painter, 20. His mother died during an abortion before he was a year old, and he doesn't know who his father was. Despite a fairly stable family life with working-class adoptive parents, he got hooked on alcohol and marijuana, and spent seventeen months in jail for armed robbery. His parole officer introduced him to Wild-cat. He dreams of attending a university and becoming a basketball star.

William (Akim) Penn, 23. Although his family was close, he had a troubled youth and spent time in jail for various offenses, including armed robbery. With few skills, no job references, a rather menacing look, and a prison record, Penn couldn't get work and turned to alcohol and welfare. He says he wants to marry the mother of his four-year old son and to create a new life for himself.

Henry Rivera, 36. An ex-addict, he has never held a regular job. He left the mother of his child to be supported by welfare. His English is rudimentary.

Carlos Rodriguez, 19. After his parents split up, his mother moved the family from Harlem to Puerto Rico. He had trouble with Spanish and was moved from fifth grade to second grade and back to fourth. He felt lost. Eventually he dropped out and returned to New York, where he had trouble finding work. Now he wants to go to college and become a pilot.

Timothy Wilson, 19. His mother was sixteen when he was born, and she and his young father "couldn't handle it," he says. He lived in four foster homes, and the experience left scars. He eventually became addicted to heroin. After serving forty-five days in jail for a mugging, Wilson went to a rehabilitation center, where he discovered his talent for music and poetry. He was reconciled to his mother, lives with her and helps provide for her in Bedford-Stuyvesant, and plans to marry a girl he met at the drug treatment center.

The members of Basic Typing-27 are scheduled to meet at nine in the morning on a Friday at the Mid-Manhattan Library on East 40th Street. Few of them have ever been to a library. Howard Smith wants them to learn to do research for a paper they will write defining what he calls "the welfare mentality," but he doesn't show up.

After huddling for forty-five minutes in the frigid lobby, the students who appeared—just five of them—decide to return to class. The five of them walk abreast down Fifth Avenue on the way back to the Wildcat Skills Training Center, on West 37th Street, seemingly unaware that they are monopolizing the sidewalk. Timothy Wilson evokes alarmed glances from pedestrians as he strides by in a black leather jacket, a black turtleneck, and an untamed Afro. Pedestrians step aside to let them pass, fixing me with a curious and sometimes startled look. As we walk west, into the garment district, the bustle of shoppers gives way to street life and black and Hispanic laborers unloading trucks and pushing racks of clothing. Here the five members of BT-27 pass unnoticed. The different reactions call to mind an observation in *Criminal Violence, Criminal Justice*, by Charles E. Silberman: "After 350 years of fearing whites, black Americans have discovered that the fear runs the other way, that whites are intimidated by their very presence."

Several minutes later they enter the familiar elevator, which creaks its way to the tenth floor of the training center. In the classroom, Howard Smith apologizes for not coming to the library, saying that his train was late. The other eleven members of BT-27 are already in the classroom; they say they forgot about the library assignment. All keep their winter coats on and complain that the room is too cold. But Smith ignores their complaints and plunges into his planned subject. He reads aloud some common assertions about welfare clients and has the students respond. Then he asks, "What do you think of the idea that welfare encourages a welfare mentality?"

"I've known one lady who told me she would have a baby every

Ken Auletta is a columnist for the *New York Daily News*. This article is excerpted from *The Underclass* by Ken Auletta (© 1982 by Ken Auletta) by permission of Random House, Inc.

year to stay on welfare," Pearl Dawson says. "That's the welfare mentality!"

"A lot of people get the idea of getting something for nothing," says Denise Brown. "I know people who live comfortably on welfare. They're satisfied with the Food Stamps they get. They know the rent is going to get paid. They have that something-for-nothing attitude."

Smith, pacing about the classroom, says, "I remember my days as a welfare recipient. The welfare center was like carnival time. We were drinking or shooting up there. I remember one time my girlfriend and I got drunk and went out and bought drugs. We shot up. The next day, we were sick. She said, 'Don't worry.' She went down to the welfare center with rags and barged in there yelling, 'God damn it, look what my baby has to play in! I didn't get my check!' She was crying. She could have put Bette Davis to shame. All recipients in the center played their part. They knew her game. But they all yelled out, 'Goddamn shame!' Half an hour later we were sitting at home shooting up with the money from the extra check. From that point on, I played the welfare game."

THE DISCUSSION continues in the hallway during a break, as the members of BT-27 smoke and sip coffee from a luncheonette downstairs. Leon Harris complains about meager welfare allowances, which in New York State were frozen from 1974 to mid-1981 at $200 a month (tax free) for a family of three. It's not enough, he says.

Gladys Miller says her after-tax Wildcat check is $83, and she gets $60 a month in Food Stamps. Her monthly rent is $150. "They clip me, I clip them," Gladys says of the welfare bureaucracy. "I go in and tell them I didn't get my Food Stamps, even though I did." As a former heroin addict, Gladys is enrolled in a methadone maintenance program. Since she no longer needs either drug, she says, she sells her methadone doses for $120 a week.

Willy Joe says, "I got a hustle—like I went to a disco for a weekend, or during the week, that's extra change." Usually he works for his brother, who organizes dances.

"I even shoot dice," Gladys Miller says.

"I usually handle a little smoke," says John Hicks.

"I don't think there's too many black people don't have a sideline," Gladys Miller says.

"I can make a hundred dollars an hour selling loose joints and bags in front of Madison Square Garden," Hicks says. "But I'm only doin' it because I need the money right now. Times gettin' hard out there, boy. They got all them guards."

"All kinds of people, too—not just blacks," Willy Joe says of hustling outside the Garden. "*Everybody*. They're professional people. They wear three-piece suits."

Gladys Miller blames government programs for inviting cheating. "Take some of the money and open up something, something of interest to alcoholics or dope fiends or methadonians, you see, so they could create jobs," she says. "But, see, the programs—I been on welfare for about seven years—are not interested in the individual, understand? They only interested in you comin' in gettin' that methadone every day. They're handing methadone out. They are supposed to make sure you swallow if they give it to you. When they take your urine, they supposed to find methadone in your urine. Now, if they come and take my urine and see that I ain't got no methadone in it—that's their fault. It's their place to tell me, 'You don't need it, get off.' But they ain't. They only interested in their jobs. Counselor has to have a certain number of patients. So that's all they interested in—the patients. Just like the Food Stamps. I'm what you call a person who takes advantage of every opportunity. Don't give me no leeway."

I ask, "What if someone said, 'Gladys, you're stealing from taxpayers by ripping off the methadone and Food Stamp programs?' "

"You look at the taxpayers that work for the system," she responds. "The government's ripping off them. They got to know I'm crooked, too. Whoever's overseeing them is also crooked."

"I got to make money the best way I know how," John Hicks says.

"Hit 'em over the head?" Gladys Miller asks.

"No, not no harm," John Hicks responds. "Plenty of ways to make money—jostling, shoplifting."

"That's the worst way," says Willy Joe.

"I tell you, that's not hurting nobody," says John, who explains that stores or wealthy individuals won't miss the money. "Not Tiffany's or nobody like that who got it like that, or people who got the money. Macy's. Mr. Macy's, for instance. Take a little—five, ten dollars—that ain't gonna hurt him too much."

John Painter, a good-looking twenty-year-old who wants to be a basketball player and consider himself a dashing dude, says his hustle—serving as an escort for women and betting about $15 a day on the numbers—doesn't harm anyone. "On a bad week, I make $75 to $100 on the numbers," he says, pulling out white receipt slips with numbers written on them.

"I deal some marijuana. Coke, when I get a chance to get it," says Henry Rivera, a pale, goateed 36-year-old ex-addict. But I don't hurt nobody, you know. I was in the street. That's where the hustling game is at for most of us drug users—hustling in the street. But at the present time I don't hustle."

I ask if hustling is necessary.

"Put yourself in our place, okay?" says Mohammed, a serene Muslim who dresses in black and who once hated whites and expressed his rage as a warlord of a Harlem youth gang. "Let's forget about middle class. You just come out of the penitentiary, or something. No job, so they place you in this program. They tell you when you first start, you'll make $110 a week. Okay, cool. You know you gotta do something to stay in the street. You know you don't wanna go back."

But the take-home pay, he complains, is not $110: "Now you're making $87 a week. You're not accustomed to it. You're accustomed to hustling. Wipe out your middle-class background. The $87 a lot of money, still. Okay. You got a place of your own, you're paying rent, light and gas, food, clothing, transportation. Now they're paying you $87, $89 a week. What do you do? How do you survive? It's a strong person that will stretch the money that far, because there's nothing to stretch. I don't hustle personally, that's against my religious code. Because of my lifestyle, I don't spend all that $87."

THEIR BREAK OVER, the members of BT-27 return to class. Howard Smith asks, "Does welfare encourage alcoholism?"

"When you're bored and don't know how to use your idle time, people want to escape from reality," Timothy Wilson says.

"It hurts," Gladys Miller says.

"Why is reality so painful?" Smith asks.

Denise Brown replies, "The reality is that the person on welfare no have what they want. No have a job. Can't get one. Might live in a slum."

"It used to hurt my father that we didn't have the things we could have," Gladys Miller says.

"They just can't deal with the everyday hassles," Harris says. "Man, doors close in their face. They think, I tried. So they get on welfare and say, 'This is not as bad as I thought.' "

"That's where the loafin' comes in," William Mason says.

"He's got no one to push him," Harris continues. "His friends say, 'Hey, man, you're right. You tried. Let's go and get high.' "

"Listen, I can't live off welfare," Pearl Dawson says. "I cannot live off this money that I am getting—that's where your family and your friends come in. That's where my idea's different from going out picking somebody's pocket."

She is asked by Smith whether it is true that some of those on welfare prefer welfare, and have more children to qualify for more benefits.

"Yes. Have baby behind baby behind baby," she answers.

"If the money is so bad and welfare is so demeaning, why should this be so?" Smith asks.

"Some people don't want to do no better," Pearl says. "They can live, month to month or week to week, on just rice and beans. First thing I do when I cash my check at the bank? I get my subway tokens so I make sure I can get here. But when you get out and start spending it, hey, it's gone. That's how much I want to get here. I buy my tokens before I buy anything else."

Smith pauses to look over the class. Except for John Painter, who is reading the sports section of the *Daily News*, and Mohammed, who is asleep, all the members of BT-27 appear to be engrossed. Smith asks, "Is there any connection between the welfare system and what happened to the South Bronx?"

Denise Brown says, "I never was able to understand why certain welfare people live under certain conditions. I was on welfare and never lived that way. It seems to me that they don't take care of their houses well, the way they would if the money was coming out of their own pocket. People come to accept the garbage and dirt in the building. I never understood that. That's the welfare mentality."

"So what you're saying is that if these people were working hard to live in this building and paying their own money, they'd take better care of the building," Smith suggests.

"I believe so," she says.

"I've seen people waiting for the mailman," William Mason says. "And then it comes time to take a leak and they don't want to go all the way upstairs. So they go right there. That leads to deterioration. That's the welfare mentality."

"They keep us in a bunch!" Gladys Miller exclaims. "They keep us together."

"We can't live on East 96th Street, because we can't afford the rent," Leon Harris says.

"You find that most Afro-Americans and blacks are contained," Timothy Wilson says. "You can find a nice five-room apartment in Bedford-Stuyvesant cheap. The streets are filthy; there are no sewers. Yet you walk around Manhattan and see all these people dressed nice."

"They don't want no niggers. It's the same with the PLO," Leon Harris explains, referring to a recent newspaper report that the residents of an affluent Manhattan cooperative rejected a PLO representative as a neighbor.

"Suppose I'm black and I don't want you 'cause you're dirty," Smith says. "Is that a fact or a myth?"

"A fact," Gladys Miller says.

"As soon as blacks and Puerto Ricans moved in, the whites moved out of Bedford-Stuyvesant," Harris says. "They moved in with their attitudes. If you think bad, it will look bad."

Smith, who is obviously building toward something, asks why this should be the case. "Are you saying we're inferior?"

"I wouldn't say we're inferior," Timothy Wilson responds, somewhat hesitantly. "But we do have vandalism and graffiti."

"Why?" Smith asks.

"It could be anger," Wilson says.

"Sometimes it's just their way of fighting back," Pearl Dawson says.

"If you tear down enough buildings, they have to move you out of the neighborhood," Harris says.

"In order to get decent housing, you must be burned out, because there's a waiting list for the public projects," says William Block. "Most people say 'Fine.' So you get a lot of fires, because they know the only way to get into these projects is by fire."

"Is THERE a connection between welfare and crime?" Smith asks.

"I was talking about this earlier today," says Timothy Wilson. "Look at the statistics of the job market. The man on the lower level is black. He can't get jobs, and if he has kids he gets on welfare. I don't think that's living. The only food in the house is mashed potatoes or bread or spaghetti. People got to feed their kids. They're sick and tired of welfare. They may pick up habits like alcoholism and start committing crime. They're doing it to live. I've seen mothers on welfare who have their kids hustle."

William Penn disagrees: "As for me, my father worked twenty years and retired. He worked for private sanitation. Me, myself, I'm saying, the welfare mentality don't inflict crime or make you go on the street. I wasn't under that mentality. I worked. My whole family worked. First time I came in contact with welfare was March 1979. That's when I came home from prison and was forced to go on welfare."

"What about buying things hot?" Smith asks.

"You don't have to be on welfare to buy things hot," Pearl Dawson says, smiling.

"To go shopping nowadays, things are very expensive," Leon Harris complains. "And if you can buy it on the street for less, you going to get it."

"Where does the hot stuff come from?" asks Smith.

"Could be your next-door neighbor," Harris replies. "You don't ask where they got it from. You want to know the price."

"How has welfare affected the family?" Smith asks.

Willy Joe says, "I feel you lose your integrity and pride. You don't have the necessities of life—nice school, nice neighborhood. Most families are not together."

"It takes your manhood away," Harris says.

"It makes you feel less than a man. They'd take my heart away before I'd go on welfare," says John Hicks, who earlier told of trying to get on welfare but being denied.

"The man's supposed to be head of the household," Gladys Miller says. "But when kids see there's not enough money they go out and hustle."

"Think of a child growing up in this environment," Smith says. "He knows nothing else—deteriorated buildings, urine in the hallways, father on alcohol who can't fulfill his role. What happens to him?"

"A lot of kids just have the attitude 'I don't care,' " William Block answers. "They sit down and think of ways how to beat the man out of welfare. For one person, welfare only allows I think $150 a month. A hundred and fifty dollars is really no money. Welfare will put you in these hotels that have all kinds of nuts in them—people from mental institutions, drug addicts. You can't keep anything of worth or value; to walk around with money in a place such as that is ridiculous. First thing you know, they got your wallet, if not worse." Block explains that he gets only $32 a month for Food Stamps and until he entered the supported-work program he received $122.85 a month from welfare. "That leaves you nothing," he says. "That brings about an idleness that brings about trouble. You always in the street, trying to get money. And if an opportunity presents itself where you can get some quick money, you just may jump into it. That will lead you to a life of crime or hurting someone."

"I've seen some children willing to pull away from welfare," William Mason says. "So many end up in the penitentiary because they want to do better. They don't have a born instinct for crime. They may be sitting home watching their mother crying because she can't afford milk. So they commit crimes to get away from it."

"I know one kid who lived in a building where he was constantly cold," Pearl Dawson says. "He set fires to keep warm."

"I know kids who did destructive things," Denise Brown says. "They broke up their rooms or didn't take care of their clothes. They did it to take out hostility."

"I think society tries to impose a welfare mentality on welfare recipients as far as the neighborhoods and the things that are presented to them," says John Painter, who has put his newspaper aside. "Something for some poor young child living in a predominantly welfare-recipient neighborhood, something he can look up to and say he wanna be, is usually gonna be something he's seen and something he knows about. Might be something in the neighborhood, somebody driving a Cadillac. Whereas somebody else might wanna be a doctor or a lawyer or something. So if people do have a welfare mentality I think it's imposed on them by society, by the things that are presented to them. Most kids in ghettos and whatnot don't think about being a doctor. They be looking forward to being something closer to the reality as they can see. In a sense, welfare mentality is thinking you gonna get something for nothing."

To prevent that attitude, he is asked, should all welfare be terminated?

"No, no, no. That's essential in today's world, where you got all this economical strife. That is an essential railing. But society plays a big part in the way the person is gonna accept it."

"You are what you eat," Timothy Wilson says, echoing the view, hinted by a few in the class, that the system, rather than the individual, is to blame. "If you eat garbage food, it affect you. If you have a kid and all he sees is pain and sorrow and garbage food, it's got to affect him. It hurts inside."

After the class breaks for lunch, I ask Smith, "What were you trying to do today?"

"I was trying to get them thinking about the effect of welfare on a person's development, on the child, on buildings, on our values. The other thing—I don't know whether you picked up on it, but there wasn't much condemnation of burning buildings and throwing garbage out the window because they feel a lot of these things are justified. . . . There's a lot of behavior in the class that is—for want of a better expression—'welfare mentality.' If you can get them thinking about welfare and its effects, then you can get them to change themselves."

8

The Underclass:
What Can Be Done?

Myron Magnet

Listen: "He made me scared, so I pulled the trigger. So feel sorry? I doubt it. I didn't want to see him go down like that, but better him than me."

"I'm gonna work forty hours a week and bring home maybe $100, $150, when I can work fifteen minutes and come back with $1,000 tax-free?"

"I ain't working for no minimum wage."

"Everybody else I knew was having babies, so I just went along."

"It just seems that everybody here is down on their luck."

The voices, reported in the press, are the voices of the underclass, and their message is that the troubles of this group at the very bottom of the American social ladder need fixing fast. For beyond the misery they occasion in underclass communities—urban knots that threaten to become enclaves of permanent poverty and vice— these are troubles that can reach out and grab the larger society by the throat. They impose costs not just in crime but also in taxes for welfare, drug programs, police, and prisons, not to mention the loss the economy suffers when an able-bodied population produces little.

Myron Magnet is a member of the Board of Editors of *Fortune* magazine. This article is abridged by permission from the May 11, 1987, issue of *Fortune* (© 1987 Time Inc.).

For business there's yet another cost: An increasing fraction of the shrinking pool of new labor-force entrants between now and the year 2000 will be underclass youths, deficient in the skills companies will need in an ever more knowledge-intensive industrial order. Add also the intangible costs: the sharpened anxiety of urban life, for instance, or the disquieting sense that something is fundamentally wrong in a rich society that allows an underclass to fester.

For all its gravity, though, the plight of this group isn't hopeless. The problems are correctable, in ways some of which are outlined below.

Who are the underclass? They are poor, but numbering around 5 million, they are a relatively small minority of the 33 million Americans with incomes below the official poverty line. Disproportionately black and Hispanic, they are still a minority within these minorities. What primarily defines them is not so much their poverty or race as their behavior—their chronic lawlessness, drug use, out-of-wedlock births, non-work, welfare dependency, and school failure. "Underclass" describes a state of mind and a way of life. It is at least as much a cultural as an economic condition.

After all, the requirements for escaping long-term poverty in America today are straightforward: (1) Finish high school, (2) get *any* job (even at the minimum wage) and stay in the labor market, (3) get married as an adult and stay married, even if it takes more than one try. "These are demanding, although not superhuman, tasks," says a report of the Working Seminar on the Family and American Welfare Policy, a group of scholars and former government officials. From a uniquely comprehensive tracking of the incomes of a wide array of people through the seventies, the group concluded that just earning a high school diploma helped keep all but 0.6 per cent of adult men and all but 2 per cent of adult women out of poverty.

Dropouts and Non-Workers

Even people familiar with the statistics on the behavior that defines the underclass feel overwhelmed when they review them. That behavior, as black social psychologist Kenneth B. Clark described it twenty-five years ago, comprises a tangle of pathologies that reinforce one another to keep the underclass imprisoned in poverty and dependence. Though free public education is the traditional vehicle of American upward mobility, 40 to 60 per cent of high school students in inner cities drop out before graduation. Though an income from full-time work at the minimum wage is enough to support a single person above the poverty line, and two such incomes can keep a family of four out of poverty, the underclass works little.

In the absence of specifically underclass numbers on all this, statistics on blacks have to serve as rough guideposts. In the fifties, black and white men participated in the labor force, either as workers or as active job seekers, at the same rate. By the late seventies black participation was 7.7 percentage points lower than white participation, a difference that statisticians deem huge. Today, only 44 per cent of black men age 16 to 24 are employed, down from 59 per cent a quarter-century ago.

In some areas that's because jobs are scarce or require skills that underclass applicants lack. But neither the statistics nor the testimony of underclass youths themselves suggests that these are the prime reasons for such extensive joblessness (though some poverty experts debate this issue ferociously). After all, black participation in the labor force declined most sharply in the economically expansive sixties, especially in that part of the decade when jobs were most plentiful. And over 70 per cent of the out-of-work inner-city black youths whom Harvard economist Richard B. Freeman surveyed in 1980 said they could easily find a job. But they generally disdained the readily available hamburger-flipper or check-out-clerk jobs as low paid or leading nowhere—even though tens of thousands of recent Asian immigrants have been finding menial jobs their gateway to the American dream. A recent ghetto renovation project in Newark, New Jersey, couldn't attract local workers at $5 to $6 an hour and ended up importing union labor from the suburbs.

In underclass communities a man who doesn't work has two principal alternatives. One is hustling—practices ranging from the shady, like hawking base-metal jewelry as silver, to the illicit but supposedly victimless, like pimping or selling drugs on the street. The other is hard-core crime, whose explosion in the sixties and seventies gave early evidence of the underclass problem. Robbery and rape rates nearly quadrupled between 1963 and 1980; burglary and assault rates roughly tripled; the murder rate more than doubled. The result is that a 12-year-old American boy has an 89 per cent chance of becoming a victim of violent crime in his lifetime, and an urban household has a 93 per cent chance of being burgled sometime during the next twenty years.

However bad the danger of robbery for middle-class whites, poor blacks get robbed four times as often, and the leading cause of death among young black men is murder. No wonder fear pervades underclass areas, deterring the law-abiding from working the late shift or attending night school.

Family Breakdown

As for the matrimonial part of the formula for escaping poverty: the breakdown of the black family that Daniel Patrick Moynihan deplored two decades ago has sharply worsened for the underclass. In 1960 three-quarters of young black men reported themselves as never having been married; that's true of 93 per cent today. But they nevertheless go on making babies. While one black child in almost six was born illegitimate in 1950, every second one was illegitimate in 1980, and today in ghettos like New York's Central Harlem, around 80 per cent of all black babies are illegitimate. Worse, two of every five of those illegitimate babies have teenage mothers, scarcely able to take care of themselves, much less raise a child.

Half of all poor families are headed by women. By definition these families provide the clientele for the largest welfare program, Aid to Families with Dependent Children, started during the New Deal to help widows and orphans but now swollen to include families lacking male heads because of divorce or illegitimacy. True, most people who go on AFDC get off fairly soon. But the long-termers—the 10 to 15 per cent who stay on the rolls eight years or more—account for over half the people on AFDC and consume more than half of all welfare payments.

The great paradox is that the underclass is a byproduct of two decades of extensive black success. Once civil-rights laws and the

War on Poverty expanded housing and job opportunities for blacks, middle-class and solid working-class inner-city minorities fled their ghettos, leaving the unsuccessful behind. Economically diverse communities turned almost overnight into homogenous enclaves of poverty.

The stranded suffered in their isolation. Their culture became one-dimensional, demoralized, with few hard-working role models to show that striving in school and getting up in the morning to go to work are normal activities that often produce success. No solid, respectable contingent remained to assert working-class and middle-class values authoritatively, keeping at least some underclass behavior in check with a good example or a sharp word. No large group of workers remained to alert youngsters to job openings and help them apply, says University of Chicago sociologist William Julius Wilson, who is black. Basic community institutions—schools, churches, stores, recreation centers—lost the support of the stable families that kept them viable, Wilson says. Crime and vandalism further hastened business flight, reducing employment and leaving little but the culture of failure, unemployment, hustling, drugs, and welfare. All these things reinforced one another, the pathological became the norm, and individual deviants solidified into an underclass.

Necessity of Welfare Reform

What is to be done? Turning the welfare system inside out is the most important first step. The current national welfare reform push, though it could end up changing only the jargon rather than the reality, so far seems to promise genuine improvement. For if the welfare system doesn't *cause* the underclass problem, it surely is one of the conditions that permit it to exist.

Among workfare systems that legislators are likely to swallow, some can be made to work, albeit gradually rather than all at once. To choose among them, just ask how well they'll reduce dependency and non-work. Black economist Walter Williams of George Mason University comments: "When we set out to help, we must always ask, 'What is the effect my helping this person will have on his helping himself?' We have ignored that question."

Says New York University political scientist Lawrence M. Mead, whose *Beyond Entitlement* is one of the landmarks of the welfare-reform debate: "One thing we should do that we haven't been doing is set standards. We talk politically only about rights, but obligations are just as important." The public has always expected people to earn a living and support their children; Mead thinks it's time the government did the same.

And not only because it is simple justice to welfare clients to treat them as citizens rather than as inferiors from whom normal behavior can't be expected. After all, how a society treats individuals on the periphery affects not only those people but also the people in the mainstream. It defines the society's values for everyone. It shows what the community requires from everyone. Exempting this class of able-bodied people from the common obligations and compromising the idea of equal treatment by the state weakens the larger society. It calls into question the sense of obligation for everybody, making all rules seem less than absolute and so easier to bend or break. And it devalues the achievement of those who fulfill their obligations. Says Harvard economist Glenn C. Loury, who is black: "We can't have the reward system such that people who are doing the right thing are told that they are chumps."

Most of all, exempting the welfare class from the common responsibilities of citizenship devalues the efforts of the respectable poor. Back in the sixties, policymakers decided that the long-term poor were victims, their poverty the result not of their own actions but of a system that was arrayed against them. For blacks, with their added burden of discrimination, that was doubly true. To hold a chronically poor person in any way responsible for his condition—and ultimately for any of his actions—was "blaming the victim," in the jargon of the time, and thus cruelly inappropriate.

Those views not only changed welfare in ways that fostered the explosive growth of the underclass; they also tended to strip the life of each poor person of its moral significance. Says Loury: "When we told all poor people that their poverty was someone else's fault and there was nothing they could do wrong, we took something away from the poor who were doing the right thing, because they are now no different from the poor who are doing wrong." That made it all the harder for the working poor to bring up their children to be as straight as they are.

Workfare strives to make able-bodied mothers, rather than the state, responsible for the support of their children. Wisconsin tries to make the fathers responsible too. Armed with a new law, the state courts now try aggressively to determine paternity, an easier task than one might think. "In the overwhelming majority of cases, the mothers know who the father is," says Irwin Garfinkel of the Wisconsin Institute for Research on Poverty. "This myth about promiscuity is a myth—and a racist myth." The courts then assess child-support payments—17 per cent of the father's income for one child—and the state attaches his paycheck to assure compliance. If he has no income now, the state attaches it whenever he starts having one. The support payment goes directly to AFDC. Says Garfinkel: "We should be getting the message across to young men that if you play the game, you have to pay."

Dealing With Crime

Young underclass men also need to get that message about crime. Because most of them aren't on welfare—a program primarily for women and children—society has no carrot to use to direct their behavior, as it does with underclass women. Nor have any voluntary programs notably succeeded into helping them into the mainstream. But to influence the most destructive feature of their behavior, society does have a stick—which it hasn't used very well. Crime has soared largely because few criminals have been made to pay a penalty. In the sixties, when crime doubled, the number of state and federal prisons fell. In the mid-seventies, the average youthful offender in the Chicago area was arrested more than thirteen times before being sent to reform school. Today, fewer than a third of those convicted of a serious crime against persons or property go to prison. Of the many who walk away with only probation, 65 per cent get picked up for similar crimes within three years.

In addition to jailing criminals, juvenile ones included, and building prisons when necessary, communities need to reassert a sense of public order in inner cities. In Cleveland a group of civic leaders has formed a Task Force on Violent Crime for just this purpose. By vigorously publicizing Ohio's eight-year mandatory sentence for using a gun to commit a crime, the group has helped lower the armed robbery rate by 30 per cent in three years. In high-crime areas, especially in housing projects, the group has helped set up mini-police stations, which have pushed down the crime rates.

Economists have a vision of man as a rational calculator, scurrying among available options to maximize gain, driven hither and yon by this incentive or that disincentive. To be sure, this way of thinking is relevant to the underclass problem. Where incentives for failure exist—welfare and the unwillingness to punish criminals are the two luminous cases in point—then of course the community has to change the calculus.

But the kind of solution most people want for the underclass is larger than this vision. The ultimate goal isn't to form a brigade of hamburger flippers and nursing-home attendants obediently going through the motions with the sullenness of Moscow street sweepers. It is to release underclass people from their imprisonment in so shrunken and self-defeating a version of humanity and to restore them to the community—to the commonplace relations and activities and aspirations that generations have deemed the source of much of life's meaning and dignity. To do that requires not a new calculus but something like a cultural revolution.

Rescuing Pre-Schoolers

What can be done for the adult underclass in this respect is meager. But children are another matter. Education can rescue them *en masse*. Not easily—the goal after all is to nurture citizens, not just raise reading scores—but it can be done.

The earlier the effort begins, the better, preferably with Head Start–like day care. One of the many welfare shibboleths is that institutional day care isn't good for AFDC kids, that it deprives them of much better nurturing from their mothers. The truth is that many underclass children, already deprived of a father, also suffer bad mothering from harried, ignorant, isolated, impoverished women, often still teenagers. That's partly why underclass children are frequently injured, burned, unimmunized; why four out of five families reported for child abuse are welfare families. That's why so many arrive at school unable to understand cause and effect, to label and classify, to see how things are the same or different, to ask a question and trust that an adult will answer helpfully, not push it aside.

For irrefutably eloquent testimony that a well-run developmental day-care program can tackle these deficiencies, look at what the High/Scope Educational Research Foundation achieved with the celebrated early-education project it began for underclass three- and four-year-olds in Ypsilanti, Michigan, in 1962. It randomly divided the children into a group of fifty-eight who went through the two-year program and a control group of sixty-five who didn't. It then followed *every* child in both groups for nineteen years after the project ended. The numbers speak for themselves: Two-thirds of the program kids finished high school, compared to half the control group. Thereafter, nearly twice as many went on to college or job training, and by age nineteen they were dramatically more law-abiding and self-supporting than the control-group kids, who were twice as likely to have illegitimate children and be on welfare.

It makes sense to proliferate programs like this, and states that require workfare for mothers with children over three should use those programs with the day-care component. Though the programs are costly, the High/Scope Foundation calculates that every dollar it spent on its target group saved society $7 in subsequent welfare, crime, lost taxes, unemployment compensation, and remediation. These programs won't work unless they have skilled staffs and rich curricula, according to High/Scope president David P. Welkart. "Otherwise we will have wasted the money," he says, "and we should have built prisons instead."

Why Have Schools Failed?

Underclass children are still salvageable by the time they get to the public schools, but the schools save few of them. After conducting so many minorities into the American mainstream, why have the schools failed with this group? Unfortunately, just as the underclass problem began to inundate inner-city schools, the same revamping spirit that was about to create the welfare mess was also depriving schools of the tools they needed to cope. "If there was a bad idea that came down the pike then, the first place it fell out was in an American school," says [then] Secretary of Education William J. Bennett.

Order and authority gave way to disruption and fear, as judges decided that school discipline was properly their business and education experts preached that orderly schools were like prisons and authoritative principals like wardens. Standards—serviceable if usually not distinguished—disintegrated as differences in test scores and promotion rates were deemed indicative only of discrimination. When pupils needed a clear statement of right and wrong, the larger culture was saying that everything is relative. When they desperately needed to be socialized into the mainstream, mainstream values were branded racist, elitist, and oppressive. Subject matter that could teach children anything larger and finer than the little they already knew was tossed overboard in favor of a specious "relevance." As people with political instead of educational agendas took over school boards, teachers lost interest and grew sullen. Civility, reading scores, basic skills, and the ability to imagine the varieties of human achievement deteriorated together.

Returning the schools to competence means reversing all this by keeping the heat on educators and school boards. Education Secretary Bennett, who has incited controversy by turning his office into a pulpit, exemplifies the appropriate kind of pressure. He holds up examples of inner-city schools that *do* work. As he describes it, the formula for success starts with an independent, high-powered principal and dedicated teachers who stick to educational basics, set high standards for achievement and conduct, articulate what's right and wrong, nurture character, try to involve parents in their children's education, and believe and preach that all children can learn. Won't all this send inner-city kids racing for the door? Thankfully, no. Bennett reports of schools he has visited: "The higher the standards, the lower the dropout rate."

State governors, too, have brought effective pressure, by, for instance, pushing through teacher competence testing and pay scales based on teacher performance, or allowing qualified applicants who haven't taken education courses to be hired for teaching jobs. Local groups—from the Allegheny Conference, an assemblage of many of Pittsburgh's business and civic leaders, to a commission set up by the Chamber of Commerce in Savannah—have begun to work closely with school boards and superintendents to monitor and upgrade their schools, through such means as giving grants to teachers and principals for innovative projects.

A booming local economy increases the leverage of such groups. It has allowed Boston business leaders to deliver on their part of a 1982 deal made with all the city's high schools, 70 per cent of whose pupils are poor and minority. Get your act together, the business leaders told the schools: if you improve your attendance and test scores, get more students to graduate and more grads to go on to college or full-time jobs, then we will give your graduates priority for our entry-level jobs. The schools adopted annual improvement plans, toughened promotion and graduation standards, went after truants, and delivered on all counts except for cutting dropouts. In 1986 Boston's big corporations hired nearly a third of the graduating class at an average wage of $5.40 an hour.

Building Self-Esteem

Remember the story of the impulsive millionaire, Eugene M. Lang? Looking down from the podium of his old grammar school in East Harlem at the sixty-one black and Hispanic sixth-grade graduates he was addressing in 1981, the technology entrepreneur realized how hollow his exhortation to have a dream and to go to college to achieve it must sound. Fat chance, the youngsters must be thinking. So on the spur of the moment he said: "If you want to go to college, you *can* go, because I promise you if you do I will give you the necessary scholarship support." Stunned silence; then pandemonium. This June [1987], more than half of them will be getting their high school diplomas, and most of the rest will graduate by December. Around two-thirds will go to college, some to top schools—this in a neighborhood where the high school dropout rate is 75 per cent and almost nobody goes to college.

But note: so far Lang hasn't spent a dime of the promised scholarship money. Money isn't primarily what accomplished this success. What these kids needed—what underclass kids need most—was to be restored to full membership in the larger community. "It's important that they grow up to recognize that they are not perpetuating the life of the pariah," Lang says, "but that the resources of the community are legitimately theirs to take advantage of and contribute to and be a part of. It's a question of outlook, of self-expectations, of knowing alternatives that are available to them."

Lang's real contribution to these kids was to get involved in their lives. He made time for them and their parents to visit his office. He took them to restaurants, the opera, the theater. He advised them, explaining what it takes to become succeed as he himself had done. He hired a full-time social worker to watch over them during the week, plan activities, iron out problems with the school, and keep them together as a mutually supportive peer group who increasingly came to feel special. "These kids have a substitute—not an ideal substitute—for what every reasonably affluent middle-class child has," he says. "I'm the same person to them that I was to my own children."

Lang has enlisted tycoons in eleven cities to take sixth-grade classes under their wings. In Detroit and Boston, black executives and professionals visit schools trying to imbue underclass youth with the goals, values, and character strength necessary to succeed. Companies including AT&T and Chase Manhattan Bank sponsor experimental job-training programs.

Not that it takes a millionaire or a corporation to give underclass kids what they need. Marva Collins does it at Westside Preparatory School, her Chicago private school for 244 mostly poor black children, a quarter of them from the notorious Cabrini-Green housing project. She teaches them everything from manners to mythology, Latin, and Shakespeare. She inculcates the lesson that if you don't work, you don't eat. "You can't decide at age 40, after having come out of prison and a drug program, that you want to be President," she tells them. "You have to plan for it, work toward it." Her 3-year-olds read at first grade level, and all—100 per cent—of her graduates go to college.

Take-Charge Tenants

Kimi Gray does it on a bigger scale at the 464-unit Kenilworth-Parkside housing project in Washington, D.C. Fed up with dirt, crime, no heat, no hot water, in 1972 Gray—as a 25-year-old welfare mother with five children—got herself elected head of the project's residents' council. She and her council immediately organized tenants into committees, started cleanup brigades, and appointed safety officers to keep front doors locked and hall lights on. Whereas Kenilworth residents once had displayed their feelings about the police by turning over their cars, Gray and her supporters fostered cooperation and got residents and police officers to view themselves as allies against criminals. After she persuaded tenants not to buy stolen goods, housebreaking plummeted. When drug pushers infested the neighborhood, she organized tenant marches to drive them out and told resident pushers and addicts that if they didn't quit in thirty days she'd have them evicted. "Crime is down 85 to 90 per cent since we started," says Gray.

She encouraged residents to take over the neighborhood PTA. Gradually their children's test scores rose, and since 1975, 582 of them have gone to college. She threatened to take some residents to court for neglecting their children. "If a white social worker said that, he'd be called racist," says Cicero Wilson, author of an American Enterprise Institute study of Gray's accomplishments. "If your neighbor says it, you can't hide behind the same slogans."

Gray took over management of the entire project in 1982, arming her efforts with economic power. She gave residents jobs, raised money to start small businesses like a screen repair shop, and used rent receipts to organize an employment agency to get tenants jobs outside the project. After living on $4,000 a year in welfare payments, residents found themselves earning $7,000 by working for Gray, perhaps supplemented by the $4,000 wage of their teenage child whom Gray had encouraged to work at McDonald's. "*That's* how people get out of poverty," says Cicero Wilson. Nearly 85 per cent of Kenilworth families were on welfare in 1972; only 20 per cent are today. Some of the project's households earn over $30,000 a year. "It works," says Wilson, "if people are required by their peers to be better."

Some poverty experts argue that the underclass problem is getting worse. Though the evidence is inconclusive, it doesn't seem that substantially more people are falling into the underclass, nor that its poverty is becoming more grinding, for Food Stamps and

Medicaid have made poverty a shade less grim than it was.

Still, every day the underclass becomes more concentrated and isolated, its pathologies deepening. But with a fast-strengthening consensus on welfare reform, a nationwide clamor to improve the schools, and impending labor shortages that make expanding and upgrading the work force crucial, this is also a moment when the beginning of a solution seems within reach.

9

Some Poverty Programs That Work

Editors, *The Washington Monthly*

Here come those acronyms again, you may be thinking, JTPA, CETA, and all the rest. There's reason to be skeptical when anyone starts up about poverty programs that work. Let's face it—most don't.

Historically, the poverty programs that have worked best have gone by different names, like good schools, a strong labor movement, and Social Security. Good schools are always good poverty programs, but they've become increasingly rare over the past twenty years. Membership in a labor union can still offer a ticket out of poverty, but those high-paying jobs that require little education are getting as rare as good public schools. And by enforcing restrictive work and membership rules, most unions seem more interested in protecting their own than in reaching out to poor non-members.

Of course the story of much of American history is the story of the best poverty program of all: economic growth. A strong economy remains an essential anti-poverty weapon. But economic growth won't do the job alone, particularly for the mostly black underclass, whose rise in the past twenty years has presented a more intractable form of American poverty. The gulf between middle-class society, black or white, and the black underclass extends

This article is abridged by permission from the June 1988 issue of *The Washington Monthly*.

113

beyond economics to values, aspirations, and behavior. It is measured in record numbers of pregnant teens, female-headed families, drug addiction, and violence, a collective social disintegration that did not exist in the ghettos of earlier generations and that responds much less readily to economic opportunity.

The programs below offer some unusual suggestions for helping the poor, from selling salsa to sneaking people into suburbs. Some of the ideas are addressed toward the problems of the black underclass, while others offer solutions more workable for less severe forms of disadvantage. They've been chosen by people trained to cast a skeptical eye on poverty promises, and their success is of a modest variety—experimental, limited, and local. In some instances, their success may consist only of failing less stupendously than similar efforts elsewhere.

While triumphs of this kind might not be ones we can savor, neither are they ones we can ignore. In considering them, it's important to think beyond the programs to the *principles* that work.

1. JOBS FOR POOR TEENAGERS

Nicholas Lemann

The idea behind Jobs for Youth/Chicago is extremely, almost off-puttingly, simple: it finds private-sector jobs for kids from poor families. The kids must be between 16 and 21, and their family income must fall below the poverty line. Practically speaking, this means that most of them come from welfare families in Chicago's black ghetto, which is the biggest in the country. Jobs for Youth, which is ten years old and funded mostly by the Labor Department (there are two loosely affiliated, and older, offices in New York and Boston), places about a thousand kids a year in jobs, and more than 90 per cent hold on to them for at least three months. If they stay on the job for six months, Jobs for Youth will help them get a better job—having an employment history is the key to getting a job with a future. Fighting poverty is supposed to be more complicated than this.

The first reason Jobs for Youth works is that its participants are self-selected. Most of them have heard of the program through word of mouth, and all of them have to be motivated enough to come to the Loop and sign up. It's easier to find jobs for people who have made a commitment to getting jobs.

Second, Jobs for Youth puts its participants through a three-week pre-employment training workshop (usually taught by a volunteer who works in business) before sending them to real employers. One of the great lessons of the past twenty years about jobs programs for poor teenagers is that they work much better if there's a buffer zone between the streets and the workplace. Job training is really a short course in acculturation for people who, first of all, are not at life's zenith of self-discipline simply by virtue of being adolescents, and second, being from welfare families, haven't spent their lives around people who work. The course at Jobs for Youth heavily emphasizes punctuality (the kids have to punch a time clock when they arrive at the office) and grooming, in addition to explaining how to deal with employers.

Third, in Chicago (as in most big cities), the private job market, while it may be bad for steelworkers, is quite good for unskilled teenagers. Employers badly need entry-level employees. Yet they are often automatically suspicious of black teenagers, especially boys. Having proved to employers over the years that its kids do well at work, Jobs for Youth in effect provides its graduates with a passport to the larger economy. It says to employers, you can feel confident that the people from our program are honest and reliable, and this helps get employers over whatever racial barriers may exist in their minds.

It's often said that many ghetto kids don't get jobs because, if all that's available is flipping burgers at McDonald's for the minimum wage, what's the use? The experience of Jobs for Youth shows that, in Chicago at least, there is more to the world of entry-level employment than fast food, and there are jobs within reasonable commuting distance of the ghettos (especially in the Loop and at O'Hare Airport). Over the past nine months, Jobs for Youth has placed only thirty kids in fast-food jobs—the bigger categories are messengers in law firms and brokerage houses, baggage handlers at the airport, and clerks in banks, and all of these start above the minimum wage. Even fast-food jobs are appealing to kids if it looks as if they'll lead to something better, which is an idea Jobs for Youth stresses heavily and can prove through its own participants' experience. Jobs for Youth also has a six-month program preparing dropouts for the high-school-equivalency exam; getting a GED (General Equivalency Diploma) can lead to college and eventually to a profession.

In the job-training business, there is a constant temptation (created in part by the hostility of labor unions to efforts to get real jobs for poor kids) to fall into a gauzy romanticism. As a result, much effort has been wasted on creating non-jobs "in the community" (this was CETA's problem—I once visited a CETA program in a housing project where the job being created was "watching cars") and on Teddy Roosevelt–style character-building exercises in which kids are taught how to rock-climb or play tennis instead of how to fill out forms. Fostering group spirit is effective but not as an end in itself. In jobs programs it works only in conjunction with getting poor kids out of the ghetto and into real jobs, and providing them with whatever instruction and emotional and practical support they need to make that considerable leap.

Nicholas Lemann, national correspondent for *The Atlantic*, is a contributing editor of *The Washington Monthly*.

2. A HEAD START ON CAREERS
Erik Payne Butler

For the past two years, Career Beginnings has served more than five thousand young people in twenty-two U.S. cities. Their "tenacity" has overcome poverty (75 per cent are officially poor), lousy urban schools (all are from cities over 100,000), and race (65 per cent are black, 18 per cent Hispanic, 8 per cent Asian). They are in neither the top 20 per cent nor the lowest 20 per cent of their class. These "middle" young people by and large get overlooked. Career Beginnings, which began in 1986, is run from the campuses of twenty-five different colleges and universities, ranging from Columbia University in New York to Rancho Santiago College in Orange County, California. It gets support from a consortium of foundations and is managed by the Center for Human Resources at Brandeis University.

Self-selection occurs: interested students apply within their high schools, which refer the most appropriate applicants to the nearby college. The program begins midway through the student's junior year and continues for two years. Career Beginnings provides remedial education when needed, and most often it is—students average two grades behind in math and reading. It offers college and career preparation plus a quality summer job, often through the Job Training Partnership Act—JTPA—and sometimes through local business groups.

Part of its secret is the group support it provides. The disadvantaged kids in the program bond as a class. They receive newsletters and design their own program T-shirts. They feel singled out and special, many for the first time in their lives.

But most important, the program offers each youngster a personal mentor, usually recruited through the local business or college community. At the University of Minnesota, mentors include Minneapolis mayor Don Fraser. The one-on-one relationship is crucial. Mentors meet with students at least once a month and stay in touch in between. They discuss work and working, assist with college applications, and help students prepare for life after high school. The best mentors act as guides, counselors, teachers, and adjunct family—not simply a role model but a real friend to one young person.

How well does it work? In our first class of 2,300, more than 95 per cent graduated from high school and completed Career Beginnings, and more than 60 per cent enrolled in college. In a recent survey 95 per cent were still enrolled in college. Our best estimates suggest that similar students not in the program would enroll in college at a rate closer to one in three, while Career Beginnings students enroll at a rate of nearly two in three.

What's more, it's cheap. Not including summer wages, the average cost per student of the two-year program is just $1,500.

Erik Payne Butler is director of the Center for Human Resources at Brandeis University.

3. JOB TRAINING WITH A PLUS
Michael Bernick

When Gloria Bestwick enrolled in the San Francisco Renaissance Center's business-machine technician training, she was determined to build a career. At 28, she was on AFDC with no job in the past year and no history of steady work. But even after she completed the fourteen-week training, her search for a job was difficult. At Xerox, which actively seeks minority women as technicians, she failed the qualifying exam. At Bell and Howell, another strong affirmative-action employer, she needed a car that she did not have. At four other office-machine companies, she was passed over for other technicians who had at least two years of experience.

After these disappointments, she kept going to job interviews, pushed on by Don Green, the director of Renaissance's vocational training. Green continued to arrange interviews, even driving her to them himself. He followed up with calls to the employers. Finally, after twelve applications, she landed a part-time job with Kennedy Business Machines, and the next year she moved into a full-time position.

Bestwick's job search shows what makes Don Green and Renaissance effective. Green, 35, came to Renaissance in 1982 after a frustrating series of jobs in the juvenile justice system ("as a counselor, which means babysitter"). He has developed classes that teach inner-city youth to repair microcomputers, office machines, and telecommunications equipment. Hundreds have taken the training over the past five years, and most of the computer stores and office-machine repair companies in the Bay area employ at least one graduate.

"By far the most important factor in training is contact with employers," Green says. He spends perhaps 30 per cent of each week either calling local employers or visiting them to stay on top of who is hiring and what skills they're looking for. He has developed the contacts and credibility that enable him to sell his product: job trainees. "I never forget I'm selling a product, and need to emphasize the customer's needs, rather than the social impact," he says.

Occasionally the transition from training to job is short and easy, but more often it is a matter of arranging many interviews, calling employers after interviews ("to show employers that our people really want the jobs"), and offering assistance to employers after placement. "It's important to us to know that we can call Don if the Renaissance graduate begins to come late or screw up," the head of a franchise computer store explains, "though often Don will take the initiative to call us and check on things."

Green also must hustle to keep trainees in class during the fourteen-week training. One day, someone will want to drop out to take a $4-an-hour fast-food job; another day, someone will be discouraged by the math skills required and decide to leave. Someone else will be threatened with eviction from an apartment, or have a fight with a girlfriend or boyfriend. Green even visits students' homes and families, in the effort to convince them that it's worth hanging in for three and a half months.

Hundreds of papers are written each year seeking to identify the elements of successful job training. These elements are not complex—strong ties with employers, a curriculum geared toward demand, motivated students, and most of all a dogged persistence in helping the students contact employer after employer in the search for work. The bigger challenge is how to attract and retain more persons like Don Green.

Michael Bernick, a San Francisco attorney, is the founder and former executive director of the San Francisco Renaissance Center.

4. THE "JOB CLUB" APPROACH
Jodie T. Allen

When I joined the Carter administration in the summer of 1977, my expectations were modest. The new President had run on a platform that called for putting more welfare recipients to work, but at no new cost to the government. No one in either the Labor Department, where I worked, or the Department of Health, Education, and Welfare took the no-new-cost requirement very seriously.

But we at Labor saw Carter's welfare reform as a chance to

redirect CETA's massive system of public-service employment away from being a quick fix for the recession toward playing a more permanent role in helping the chronically unemployed. Our idea was to attack poverty by providing work, rather than welfare. We knew enough about job programs not to make the usual rosy predictions about converting "tax-eaters to tax-payers." We didn't even assume participants would move from our public jobs into private ones any faster, but in the meantime at least they'd be working for their income.

This honesty turned out to be bad strategy. One reason is that Congress *likes* to be courted with inflated predictions of welfare dollars saved and lives transformed. But it also turned out that our skepticism was not fully justified.

One of the features of our job program was an eight-week waiting period before a recipient could claim a public job. The purpose was to prevent unemployed people who would otherwise find a regular job in a few weeks from using up one of our expensive subsidized jobs instead. The waiting period was very unpopular among the administration's liberal supporters, who regarded it as heartless. (Never mind that waiting didn't make anyone worse off than he currently was without any job program at all.) At least we should give them some help in looking for a job, and maybe get them a bit more ready, said the critics.

I was not thrilled by the idea of allocating scarce money to more of the same old job-preparation assistance that had done so little in the past. So I was dubious when my staff brought in a starry-eyed psychologist named Nathan Azrin who said he had developed a "Job Club" that would find unsubsidized jobs for two out of three of our welfare clients in a matter of weeks. Still, we needed something, and the price was right—which is to say cheap.

The next thing I knew the thing was working. Up in Lowell, Massachusetts, where the electronics industry was just starting to boom, Azrin's club was siphoning off 90 per cent of participants into stores and factories before our subsidized-job placers got a crack at them. Even in rural Missouri more than three out of five were finding jobs quickly.

One key ingredient in Job Club success was a meticulously

trained, highly enthusiastic staff. Another was that welfare clients had to take the initiative in finding the jobs. In traditional programs, professional manpower specialists would pronounce the client either "job ready," in need of further training or other aid, or a hopeless case to be returned to the welfare rolls. The Job Club approach left the job-readiness decision to the labor market.

Participating in the program was obligatory for many Job Club clients, a feature that many felt was helpful in overcoming long-term shyness about approaching employers. (But the really tough cases—adults with chronic drug, alcohol, physical, or behavioral problems, of which there are many—didn't come to the program at all.) Most clients were eager to test the waters.

Job Club trainers, working primarily with small groups, taught their clients to search their pasts and remember experiences that might suggest a marketable skill—a part-time job after school, a school subject or sport done well, success in organizing school or volunteer activities, help provided to neighborhood kids. The trainers encouraged clients to begin feeling self-reliant.

The Job Club method of finding jobs was a striking departure from accepted practice. In the traditional model, "job-development specialists" typically put in a call to one of the handful of firms they have scored some success with in the past and ask if they can send over a welfare recipient who might work out. But sending a job-seeker out with a label reading "Hire me, I'm on welfare" is a sure turnoff for most employers, a turnoff that even bribing employers with tax credits or bounties can rarely overcome. The Job Club approach teaches clients how to find a job for themselves: how to use a phone book to find likely employers, how to follow up, and so on. Then participants set to work with a bank of phones— making calls, following up on leads, going out to interviews, coming back and reporting to their fellow job-seekers.

No doubt the success rate of the pilot projects would have fallen as caseloads grew and job openings grew scarcer. But even at half the rate, the success would have been phenomenal for this clientele. Although the Reagan administration threw out the pilot projects along with the rest of CETA, some Job Clubs still exist. Perhaps with the growing interest in rescuing welfare recipients from dependency, the Job Clubs will be given a chance to make a more lasting contribution to this effort.

Jodie T. Allen is deputy editor of the *Washington Post*'s Sunday "Outlook" section.

5. HELPING WOMEN ENTREPRENEURS

Roger J. Vaughan

Two sisters in St. Paul, Minnesota, had little income but a valuable asset: a prized family recipe for salsa. After a bank denied their application for a $10,000 loan to go into business, the sisters were referred to the Women's Economic Development Corporation. With WEDCO's help and hard work, they prepared a more realistic plan, returned to the bank, and received a loan nearly twice the size of their original request. Now they are shipping more than half a million dollars' worth of salsa each year.

WEDCO is a non-profit corporation in St. Paul that assists women entrepreneurs. In the four years since its doors opened, 3,500 women have been helped, 644 new businesses created, and 400 existing businesses expanded, at a failure rate below 5 per cent. Most striking, 67 per cent of the women starting or expanding businesses had incomes below $15,000, and 63 per cent were single heads of households. WEDCO's businesses are diverse but heavily weighted toward retail and craft businesses. They also include a firm that leases space to occupational therapists, a book distributor, a custom upholsterer, a wood carver, and a pest-control firm.

WEDCO is the brainchild of four women entrepreneurs who knew that women face special problems if they try to start businesses: a lack of the networks that men can draw on for advice, lower self-esteem, and little respect from bank loan officers. At the same time, the First Bank of Minneapolis realized the advantages of a place to refer loan applicants whose business plans had potential but needed work. Started with bank money and foundation grants, WEDCO today has a staff of ten and operates on a $490,000 annual budget. It covers about one-third of its expenses from earned revenues, which include fees charged to clients and the sale of "how to" workbooks. WEDCO teaches would-be entrepreneurs everything from marketing, management, and finance to self-confidence. It does not attempt to screen winners and losers because too many improbable ideas have proved successful—including a pet modeling agency! Instead, between visits, clients must complete homework assignments. This weeds out those who cannot convert a vague idea into a viable business plan.

WEDCO also offers two last-resort finance programs funded by banks and by foundations. In three years, 110 loans have been advanced, ranging from $350 to $20,000. Of the more than $700,000 loaned, only $10,000 is in default.

The secret of WEDCO's success might seem simple but is not; the program will probably prove very hard to clone. WEDCO is run by experienced and hard-working professionals and is directly accountable to its funding sources—private, for-profit banks and foundations. As investors in WEDCO's own loan funds and as board members, the banks weigh the success of the program more carefully than most state legislatures oversee state agencies. The track record of state and local loan programs that assist small and minority-owned businesses is bad enough to give pause to those who might want to rush to subsidize a local version of WEDCO.

Entrepreneurship is certainly not a way for all able-bodied people to escape welfare. But one displaced worker in eight who has found work over the past decade has done so by creating his own job. WEDCO has proved that entrepreneurship can work for poor women.

Roger J. Vaughan is an economic consultant based in Portland, Maine.

6. JOB TRAINING AT COMMUNITY COLLEGES

Dale Russakoff

In 1983, unemployment had moved like a blight through Pittsburgh and surrounding Allegheny County. More than 95,000 men and women, or one in seven workers, had lost their jobs—not only as steelworkers but as restaurant workers, policemen, janitors, secretaries, clerks, and skilled laborers whose tasks were tied to the health of steel. The sheer breadth of the problem spawned a collective consciousness that led to a remarkable job-training effort on the five campuses of the Community College of Allegheny County.

In 1983–84, more than 7,000 unemployed men and women enrolled in the college to train for a range of jobs, with their expenses paid by county, state, and federal governments. It was the largest project of its kind in the United States, and it has since been studied by observers from thirty-seven countries. It was also one of the most successful. In three follow-up surveys the college conducted, the most recent in April 1987, almost 80 per cent of the participants had found new jobs and remained in them. Of those, 84 per cent said their new jobs grew from the college training; only 16 per cent said the jobs were similar to the ones they had lost.

Each of these men and women had held a job before, but many had been out of work more than two years and had come to view themselves as hard-core unemployed in a region where the competition for jobs was great. Some stayed a semester, some three years. They emerged as nurses, chefs, landscapers, gardeners at downtown buildings, computer technicians and programmers, office clerks, and fast-food franchisers: most of the job categories reflected the shift from a manufacturing to a service economy.

Compared to federal job-training administrators, county officials proved unusually flexible. Participants had to be county residents who, as of spring 1983, had been eligible for unemployment compensation within the past eighteen months. To enroll, they simply had to apply to the college. By contrast, enrollment in the federal JTPA (Job Training Partnership Act) program required more than a dozen kinds of documents, including income stubs going back six months, proof of family size, and other papers that few people have at the ready.

Perhaps most important was the county's decision to vest its effort in a community college. Many of these schools have become de facto vocational training centers, with courses closely keyed to the needs of the local economy. Faculty members, unlike their colleagues at most liberal arts colleges, are accustomed to dealing with the pragmatic concerns of diverse, largely adult student bodies. Another key feature was that the program was run by counselors, not job-training "experts." Uncomfortable with the idea of economic forecasting, they resisted the temptation to direct workers into what seemed "hot" careers, such as robotics—in retrospect, a good move. Each student chose his or her own direction. Laid-off workers, in interviews, said having this choice was an important step for them toward taking charge of their destiny, after feeling at the mercy of economic forces.

"We were dealing with very disillusioned people and we did not want to make promises we couldn't keep" said Barbara Parees, the college's head of educational services. "When they came in, we said: 'We do not have jobs. We are not offering you jobs. We are offering you a chance to become educated.' "

Dale Russakoff is a reporter on the national staff of the *Washington Post*.

7. A Development Bank for the Ghetto
David Osborne

The nation's best jobs program for the poor, in my opinion, is not a jobs program. It is not even a government program. It is a private development bank on Chicago's south side called the Shorebank Corporation. Shorebank consists of a bank, a real-estate development, a venture capital fund, and a community-development corporation. It occupies neither the public sector nor the private sector but a "third sector" in between. It is the flagship of a growing movement to apply entrepreneurial methods to social problems.

The story began in the late 1960s, when a young Chicago banker named Ron Grzywinski seized upon an offer by then state treasurer Adlai Stevenson III to deposit state funds in banks that loan to minority business people. Grzywinski, who then owned a small bank near the University of Chicago, recruited two black activists and a young woman fresh out of graduate school. With no background in banking, they outshone Chicago's major banks. Their success got them thinking about the potential impact an aggressive bank could have on a black ghetto. Grzywinski took a leave of absence, raised $800,000 from foundations and philanthropists, borrowed $2.4 million more, and bought South Shore Bank.

As they groped for a strategy to turn South Shore around, it became clear that the key was rehabilitating the apartment buildings that housed 70 per cent of the neighborhood's 80,000 people. When buildings are abandoned in a neighborhood like South Shore—as they were in rising numbers throughout the seventies— the empty halls become targets for arson and hangouts for junkies. Crime skyrockets, and law-abiding residents flee. Black neighborhoods all over Chicago's south side have been depopulated in precisely this way.

South Shore Bank set out to reverse the downward spiral by doing what no other financial institution in Chicago would do: giving mortgages on ghetto apartment buildings. By 1987 it had made more than $35 million in mortgage and rehab loans on more than 200 buildings—close to a quarter of all apartment buildings in South Shore. The impact was dramatic. There are still some pockets of decay, but, driving the tree-lined streets, one also sees elegant courtyard buildings that would fit well into the tonier north side neighborhoods.

Meanwhile, Shorebank's community-development corporation has trained hundreds of residents for jobs, provided remedial education, created a small-business incubator to help new firms survive, and created a program to help neighborhood women (including welfare recipients) go into business for themselves. Shorebank's real-estate firm recently broke ground on an eight-acre shopping center. In the process, thousands of people have found work. But more important, the community fabric now reinforces the work ethic.

This is one key to Shorebank's success: instead of attacking only one of the community's problems, it has attacked on a broad front. Shorebank's other secret is that it does not spend money—it *invests*. The typical government program, no matter how well intentioned, provides money or sevices to poor people simply because they are deserving. In contrast, Shorebank invests in people because it believes they can succeed in the marketplace. If an applicant does not have that capacity—whether he or she wants to start a business, buy a building, or simply get job training—Shorebank will not invest. This is not a strategy that will work in every inner-city neighborhood. Some of our ghettos are too far gone. Nor is it an argument for expecting business to solve social problems. There is simply not enough easy profit available in a community like South Shore for a traditional bank or developer. There must be some subsidy, and there must be a commitment to more than the bottom line. This is where government might come in—to provide some of this capital and inspire some of the talent. John Kennedy inspired a generation to enlist in the Peace Corps, VISTA, and the War on Poverty. Another president could do the same with an anti-poverty strategy built on the third-sector model.

David Osborne is the author of *Laboratories of Democracy*, published in 1988 by Harvard Business School Press.

8. CASE STUDIES PLUS HARD NUMBERS
Ken Auletta

One terrific anti-poverty program I've encountered employs no teachers, counselors, or job-skill instructors. It doesn't perform miracles—like luring dropouts back to school, or helping to instill self-esteem, or training ex-addicts for the world of work. It isn't located in an inner-city slum. In fact, the Manpower Demonstration Research Corporation doesn't run poverty programs. It analyzes them.

Located on Manhattan's Park Avenue, the non-profit, Ford Foundation–inspired MDRC specializes in information. No university or government agency has done more extensive studies of subsidized employment programs, of teen parenting efforts, of workfare and welfare reforms. When the federal government shifted away from the hard-core underclass, MDRC entered into contracts with state and local governments and organizations to evaluate poverty programs.

One clear lesson their work imparts is the need to avoid oversimplification. We are not dealing with a homogenized group of people whom we can label *poor* and for whom we can prescribe a single remedy. No simple answers will do, whether in the form of conservative bumper stickers that shout Individual Responsibility or liberal bumper stickers that shout Government Responsibility. What we need is a synthesis.

MDRC's twin approach to research couples hard numbers with very human case studies. The hard numbers guard against misleading anecdotal evidence. But the case studies guard against the sweeping generalizations of purely statistical approaches. Individuals in poverty have an assortment of problems that extend beyond mere lack of income and can include illiteracy, lack of self-confidence, and lack of emotional support. We need to distinguish between the underclass and those who are only temporarily poor, between those with behavioral as opposed to just income woes. The nuanced approach of MDRC's research suggests the need for more customized anti-poverty programs.

Of equal import, MDRC's respected analysis might unlock the secret to capturing the support of the American people. The public might gain confidence from hearing some of the many success stories of the temporary poor, stories that are often dwarfed by the failure stories of the more recalcitrant underclass. Perhaps people would gain new insight into how painfully difficult it sometimes is to reach the underclass. If we treat voters as if they have a consumer right to know what they're getting for their money, perhaps they will return the compliment in the form of greater patience and understanding.

Ken Auletta, a columnist for the *New York Daily News*, is the author of *The Underclass*.

9. Evacuating Families from Ghettos
Nicholas Lemann

There are certain liberal ideas that we've all taught ourselves to believe can't possibly work. One of these is the idea that government agencies could move some poor black families from the inner-city ghettos to the mostly white suburbs, where the schools are better, the streets are safer, and, these days, the jobs are more plentiful. Just mentioning it brings visions of rocks thrown through windows and kids tormented by their classmates. But there is such a program in Chicago, and it has moved 3,500 families from ghetto public-housing projects into suburbs since 1976, with considerable success. It is so popular that it gets 2,000 applicants in an annual one-day sign-up period. Relatively few of the families moved have experienced harassment, many who were unemployed in the city have found jobs in the suburbs, and in surveys the overwhelming majority say they are much happier with their kids' schools now than they were in the city.

The program was begun in 1976 by the Leadership Council for Metropolitan Open Communities, an organization founded (as part of a 1966 peace treaty between Martin Luther King and Mayor Richard Daley) to promote residential desegregation. The Gautreaux Program is named for a woman who sued the Chicago Housing Authority for operating segregated housing and won; the Leadership Coucil runs it as part of the settlement between CHA and the plaintiffs. Only residents of segregated housing projects in Chicago (most of the housing projects in Chicago *are* segregated) are eligible for the program. The Leadership Council places them in other housing, mostly in the suburbs, and gets them HUD Section 8 rent subsidies to pay for it.

In Chicago, as elsewhere, there is a certain amount of resident pride to be found in every housing project. Even the infamous Cabrini-Green has residents who are ardently trying to keep it from being torn down the way the even more infamous Pruitt-Igoe was in St. Louis in the seventies. But the truth is that most people in housing projects desperately want to get out. In particular, the out-of-control gang crime makes them want to leave; in general, the poor inner-city neighborhoods where most housing projects are located have long since ceased being able to provide their residents with education, employment, and a community life. The way to move up in the ghetto is to move out of it.

One reason the Gautreaux Program works is that it's an una-bashed practitioner of "creaming," which means helping only the most motivated and most "together" people. Creaming is politically incorrect, but it works. As a voluntary program, Gautreaux gets a self-selected group of applicants who are on the average better educated and more likely to be employed than most residents of housing projects. In choosing among the applicants, the program engages in practices that used to be part of the standard operating procedure of public-housing projects but were dropped in most places in the sixties for being, again, politically incorrect: as the brochure for applicants says, "Only families with acceptable house-keeping habits, credit, rental, family and personal histories and those with the minimum resources for moving will be referred." Gautreaux even uses such appurtenances of the much reviled "social worker mentality" as home visits.

It takes extraordinary strength for a poor black single mother to move her kids into a middle-class white neighborhood far away from anyone she knows, where they will have to endure, if not racial taunts, at least a lot of funny looks. On the suburban end, the program firmly lines up the cooperation of private landlords in advance. Most important, it operates in quasi-secrecy. The landlords and the families moving out from the projects are under strict instructions not to tell anybody how the families got there; they are just the new folks who happened to move into the apartment house.

Nicholas Lemann, national correspondent for *The Atlantic*, is a contributing editor of *The Washington Monthly*.

10

The Business Alternative

Judson Bemis

For decades, we have assumed that solving the problems of needy Americans requires an endless one-way flow of resources. Thus unemployment, crime, drug abuse, poverty, and mental illness have all consumed billions of public and private dollars. But what would happen if we were to change our expectations—if we could learn to see human services as business opportunities? What if we could transform resource-users into resource-producers? Is it possible to think and act as entrepreneurs in the human-services sector?

I think so. I think the delivery of human services can be susceptible to a *market* approach, with measurable returns in a reasonable amount of time, without reducing quality. In fact, it is already starting to happen. In the last few years, more than two hundred small businesses have been launched by human-services entrepreneurs. Numerous non-profit agencies have converted to for-profit status or have opened for-profit subsidiaries. Dozens of local and state governments have been issuing contracts to for-profit human-services companies.

Human-services entrepreneurs are finding ways to merge profit motives with moral imperatives. For many of them, however, profit is not the principal objective; if it were, they would probably pick

Judson Bemis is the chairman of the Alpha Center for Public/Private Initiatives in Minneapolis, Minnesota. This essay is abridged and reprinted by permission of the author. It originally appeared in the June 1988 issue of *Imprimis,* a publication of Hillsdale College, Michigan.

131

an easier business. The for-profit approach is a tool for extending their services to more and more people.

It shouldn't be surprising to see for-profit vendors delivering human services. After all, more than a hundred municipal services are today performed by contract, among them snow removal, waste disposal, fire protection, and recreation. At every level, governments are still deciding which services to provide, but many of them no longer produce and deliver them through public employees. This same strategy in human services gives public officials another way to leverage their limited resources, to save money or to spend it smarter without relinquishing responsibility for assessing local needs, setting standards, and monitoring performance.

Some Successful Enterprises

Let me offer a few examples of the kinds of human-services companies that have appeared in recent years.

America Works. Three years ago, in Massachusetts, Peter Cove founded a company called America Works, basing it on a subsidized non-profit model. The company trains welfare recipients and places them in permanent jobs in the private sector. More than 90 per cent of the welfare recipients in this country are women who are single heads of households. In one state, the average America Works program beneficiary has several children and lives on $300 a month, often in a dwelling without adequate heat or light. During its first year of operation in that state, America Works removed 430 people from the welfare rolls.

Two-thirds of the company's revenue comes from governmental agencies, one-third from companies that employ the trained graduates. The companies have a "try before you buy" option. The welfare recipients remain employees of America Works for as long as five months until employers are satisfied they'll work out; only then are they transferred to the payrolls of the companies.

Some of the money America Works receives from the government is diverted from "workfare" programs, AFDC, and the like. The government may not be saving money, but it is channeling dollars to a program that leads people towards self-sufficiency and eventually off the welfare rolls instead of maintaining them in a state of dependency. It takes about $4,800 in new government spending to put one person through the America Works program. This amount is returned to the state in eight months because AFDC payments, Medicaid, Food Stamps, and other assistance are no longer necessary. After that, the state receives a return of 750 per cent on its investment every year for each person who goes through the program successfully.

CareerWorks. Seven years ago, eleven people left the Chrysler Learning Center in Detroit to begin providing customized job training for the economically disadvantaged. CareerWorks now has regional training centers in twelve cities around the nation teaching job skills in more than thirty-five categories. Graduates include clerical workers, robotics technicians, bank tellers, security guards, and mechanical drafters. Twelve thousand people have been placed by CareerWorks during the past five years, saving the federal government more than $46 million in transfer payments.

VisionQuest National. Thirteen years ago three corrections officials, frustrated with the system, quit their jobs and convinced a juvenile-court judge to entrust them with five multiple offenders. Today, VisionQuest National has 550 employees, has contracts with social-service officials in seventeen states, and generates annual revenues of more than $20 million. VisionQuest runs twelve camping programs, including Wagon Trains, Tall Ships, Wilderness Journeys, and Bicycling. Students remain in the program for more than a year and, despite recent controversy over the program's effectiveness, a Rand Corporation study shows that VisionQuest has at least as good a recidivism rate as the rate for lockup facilities and costs the taxpayers far less.

Educational Clinics, Incorporated. According to the Michigan State Department of Education, more than 60 per cent of Detroit's teenagers are high school dropouts. Chicago loses 53 per cent; Oregon, 32 per cent; Washington, 30 per cent. Educational Clinics Incorporated provides remedial training for high school dropouts in Washington and California. These are 15- to 19-year-olds, for the most part tough kids with tough problems. Most come from low-income, single-parent families. Many of them have been physically or sexually abused. After a three-month stay in the ECI program, according to an independent follow-up study conducted three years later, 75 per cent had either gone back to school or received their GED (General Equivalency Diploma) and were half as likely as those who hadn't gone through the program to wind up on the criminal rolls.

In addition, of high school dropouts who now hold full-time jobs, those trained originally by ECI were earning, on the average, five years later, $2,100 more per year than their counterparts and paying $568 more in taxes. ECI has trained more than 4,500 students, and the program has been so successful that legislators in both California and Washington have enacted laws to permit the use of public funds for tuition.

Entrepreneurs have started other small businesses in areas such as home care for the elderly and disabled, placement programs for unwanted children, alternative sentencing for the criminal-justice system, curative programs for substance abusers. Others have started companies that employ the disadvantaged. In Minnesota, a company reserves half its jobs for ex-prisoners; in Kansas, a company employs current prisoners outside the walls; in Wisconsin, a company employs people with mental handicaps.

Ending "Either/Or"

At the Alpha Center for Public/Private Initiatives in Minneapolis, which I serve as chairman, we have broken the human-services industry down into fifty-three categories and subcategories of need. We have found small companies working in each area. Some are former non-profits; many are independent ventures started by individuals who had been government, corporate, or non-profit workers. All of them are self-sufficient organizations that serve the disadvantaged without depending on philanthropy or public subsidy. They may receive fees from the public sector for services rendered, but they no longer depend on grants or seed money for their operations.

The benefits of this new approach, the third alternative, fall into at least five categories:

First, investment capital has made it possible to take something that works and deliver it to more people faster. Entrepreneurs don't have to wait for charity or government subsidy before they can attract loans or sell equity in order to start a new venture, or introduce a successful model into another city or county.

Second, working in a for-profit enterprise, entrepreneurs and their employees have a personal financial stake in its success or failure. Typically, government and non-profit employees receive a flat salary. There is no financial incentive to do more or better and no financial penalty for doing less or worse. In a small business, however, careers rise or fall with the success or failure of the company, and innovation may flourish.

Third, by developing for-profit subsidiaries, non-profits can reduce their dependency on philanthropy or government subsidy and stabilize their sources of revenue. While some organizations act only because they are in a crisis, others do so because they have proven programs that could be delivered to more people if sufficient expertise and capital were available.

Fourth, contracting with for-profit vendors has enabled government agencies to leverage their limited financial and labor resources without (and this is very important) relinquishing responsibility for setting standards and monitoring performance. Agencies contracting human services have saved money, improved service quality, made services available to more people, limited the size of local government, and increased the managerial capabilities of in-house staffs.

Fifth, the for-profit approach has given foundations and corporate grant-makers a way to extend the use of their funds. By helping some recipients achieve self-sufficiency, they are able to redirect resources to other groups in subsequent years.

Answering the Skeptics

To skeptics, all the positive examples in the world will not make the third alternative palatable. Many of them believe it is not possible to mix compassion with profits, that the profit motive means quality will suffer and that people who really need the services won't be able to afford them. They also believe it's simply illegitimate to make money "off the backs of the poor."

I find these doubts fundamentally puzzling. It is not illegitimate for a grocery store to charge for a can of soup, for a carpenter to charge for building a house, or a department store to put a price tag on a pair of jeans. Food, shelter, and clothing are all basic human requirements, yet we see nothing illegitimate in making money from providing them. Profits are necessary to keep the grocery stores, the carpenters, and the department stores in business. They are the source of new products, new jobs, new ways to provide services.

As for concerns about quality and the truly needy, those objections can be met if government plays its proper role in the partnership—if a government agency writes a contract that addresses the issues head-on, a contract that is properly structured and monitored. I can't emphasize enough the importance of forging a partnership between the public and private sectors. And a tightly written contract, with proper government supervision, can also ease the fears of people who believe the entry of for-profit companies means government will lose control of human-services delivery, that we will open the door to waste, fraud, and abuse, or that costs will escalate dramatically.

In evaluating a particular way of delivering human services there are three criteria: (1) Effectiveness: does it meet the needs of individual recipients and of the local community? (2) Equity: is the service available and affordable to those who need it most? (3) Efficiency: how much output will be generated for each unit of input? What we are searching for is the best combination of resources—the best of the non-profit world, the best of the for-profit world, the best of the public sector. There is more than enough room for all of us. We need to merge our resources to find new ways of meeting our society's needs.

Index of Names

Aid to Families with Dependent
Children (AFDC), 23–24, 26,
28, 30, 32, 39–41, 44, 47,
53, 57, 60, 63, 66, 74–76, 78,
102, 105–6, 118, 132–33
Allegheny Conference, 108
Allegheny County, Community
College of, 123–24
Allen, Jodie T., 119
Alpha Center for Public/Private
Initiatives, 131, 134
American Civil Liberties Union
(ACLU), 49
American Federation of State,
County, and Municipal Employ-
ees, 34
America Works, 132–33
Arizona, 37
Atlantic, The, 20, 43
Auletta, Ken, xii, 20, 24, 85, 127

Babbitt, Bruce, 37
Bane, Mary Jo, 20, 37, 62–63, 66
Bemis, Judson, xiii, 131
Bennett, William J., 108
Berger, Peter, 11
Bernick, Michael, 118
Beyond Entitlement (Lawrence Mead),
37, 104
Black Boy (Richard Wright), 15
Brandeis University, 30, 41
Burns, Arthur, 30
Bush, George, ix, xi
Butler, Erik Payne, 116

Cabrini-Green housing project, 110,
129

California, xi, 23, 25, 27, 34, 53, 76,
134
Career Beginnings, 116–17
CareerWorks, 133
Carlyle, Thomas, 2
"CBS Reports," 20
Cherbourg, Royal Academic Society
of, 9, 11
Chicago, 13, 62, 133
Chicago Housing Authority, 129
Chicago, University of, 16, 28, 37,
103, 125
Chrysler Learning Center, 133
Churchill, Winston, 5–6
Clark, Kenneth B., 19, 100
Cloward, Richard, 53
Collins, Marva, 110
Commission, Royal, 3
Comprehensive Employment and
Training Act (CETA), 34–35,
48, 69, 113, 116, 120–21
Congress, ix, 25, 42, 66, 69, 120
Cove, Peter, 132
Criminal Violence, Criminal Justice
(Charles E. Silberman), 89

Daley, Richard, 129
Dark Ghetto (Kenneth Clark), 19
Dash, Leon, 20, 43–44
Deukmejian, George, 27
Drescher, Seymour, 10–11
DuBois, W. E. B., 15

Earned Income Tax Credit, 30, 38–
39
Economic Illusion (Robert Kuttner),
37

137